Woodcarving Patterns from Around the World

E. J. Tangerman

Sterling Publishing Co., Inc.   New York

Library of Congress Cataloging-in-Publication Data
Tangerman, E. J. (Elmer John), 1907–
    Woodcarving patterns from around the world / E. J. Tangerman.
        p.   cm.
    Includes index.
    ISBN 0-8069-6698-X
    1. Wood-carving—Patterns.   2. Wood-carving—United States—
Patterns.   I. Title.
TT199.7.T38   1989
731.4'62—dc19   89-31163
                                                                      CIP

        3   5   7   9   10   8   6   4   2

Copyright © 1989 by E. J. Tangerman
Published by Sterling Publishing Co., Inc.
387 Park Avenue South, New York, N.Y. 10016
Distributed in Canada by Sterling Publishing
% Canadian Manda Group, P.O. Box 920, Station U
Toronto, Ontario, Canada M8Z 5P9
Distributed in Great Britain and Europe by Cassell PLC
Artillery House, Artillery Row, London SW1P 1RT, England
Distributed in Australia by Capricorn Ltd.
P.O. Box 665, Lane Cove, NSW 2066
Manufactured in the United States of America
All rights reserved

Sterling ISBN 0-8069-6698-X Paper

Table of Contents

Fig. 1. King Solomon, a detail on the right side of the base of the altar of the Seven Sorrowing Marys in St. Nicholas Church, Kalkar, West Germany, shows the artistry achieved by the German master carvers. The altar was carved in 1522 by the lower-Rhine master Kendrick Douermann. Photo courtesy German Information Center, New York.

Introduction

For the past 30 years, I have been visiting those parts of the world where wood-carving is still done extensively, originally as an offshoot of my work and for 20 years since I retired as a sort of hobby. These visits have led me to some general conclusions and, I suppose, to some personal biases as well. I found, for example, that our modern technology and industrial development have caused a corresponding decline in crafts around the world. As our methods of production and our gadgetry have permeated other countries, those countries have established their own manufactories, and the native carvers go to work in them because they have innate skills that command premium salaries—far more than they could make as wood-carvers. So the craft is abandoned, as it was here earlier in the century, when we had to import European carvers to do such architectural carving as was needed.

What's more, wherever there are buyers, there soon develops a coterie of sellers and a sort of industry to supply the sellers. Tourism has become big business in many parts of the world, and tourists buy "artifacts" (the genteel word for souvenirs of more or less value—call it an artifact and it sells for twice or three times as much as a souvenir). And as soon as an appreciable market develops for a particular artifact, somebody begins its manufacture in quantity—there, or elsewhere where labor is cheaper.

Thus Alaskan "hand-carved" bears and other objects in several kinds of stone are now turned out on machines in Seattle, some of which employ emigré Eskimos so they can claim "Made by Eskimos" on the label. Wooden bears are made in Korea and by Ainu aborigines in Japan. Eskimo ivory carvers emigrate to the cities where power is available to operate rotary power tools.

In Europe now, carving is done largely in pockets such as Brienz in Switzerland, Oberammergau and Tribourg in Germany, a spot or two like the Tyrol in Italy and the Dalarna area in Sweden, villages in Poland and the U.S.S.R., and similarly localized areas in Spain, Poland, and Greece.

Fig. 2. This fake miniature totem pole comes from Canada, is a pendant in some sort of composition, and is typical of a number of pieces of "carved stone" at popular prices which are actually mere castings.

Fig. 3. "Kräxenträger aus dem Stammhaus Lang sel Erben" in Oberammergau, West Germany, is a life-size modern statue of a toy peddler of several centuries back. He carried his wares on display as he trudged from village to village. During medieval times, this was the standard way to sell woodcarvings.

Even in this country, professional carvers doing major architectural work are rare; carving is slow, time-intensive, and thus expensive compared with mass produced items in these cost-conscious days. We do have traditional woodcarving "pockets" like St. Pièrre-Port Julie in Canada, and Brasstown and other areas in the Southern Highlands of the U.S.A., but they are uncommon.

In Oberammergau there are several companies operating multi-spindle duplicators who supply blanks to other shops for "hand-carved" finishing. In Kenya, Bali, Japan, Nepal, India, China, Sri Lanka, West Sumatra, and the U.S.S.R., among others, there are more of these "factories" turning out carvings of standardized types. The equipment and facilities may be of the crudest, and the individual carvers may have considerable freedom in adapting designs, but they are still working more or less for a factor who acts as their selling agent. He may get a definite percentage on a price they set, or he may set prices, or he may even run a sweatshop, depending upon demand, local laws, and the state of the economy. In Mexico, there are certain carving villages where entire families take part, each member doing what he or she can toward a final product. In Mexico also, when the Seri Indians of Sonora made a success of their stylized ironwood carved animals, the mestizos started up a factory in Hermosillo to turn

Figs. 4 and 5. This small head of a jaeger or huntsman is very intricate and typical of the finer modern work done in Oberammergau, West Germany. It is a high-relief silhouette, tinted and flat on the back so it can be hung.

Figs. 6 and 7. These Kenyan animals are thin-bodied and range up to 4 in. (102 mm) long. They are typical of third world "factory" production—standardized and hastily done.

Thin upper body to ¼"

Lion- ⁷⁄₁₆ × 1 × 3¼"

spots painted

Leopard- ½ × 1½ × 3½"

African animals are "tourist" items, cheap but crude carving

Boar- ⅜ × 1 × 2½"

Rhino ⅜ × 1⅜ × 2¼"

VELDT ANIMALS
Vertical-grain, striped -Kenya

Fig. 8. Two llamas flank an alpaca. The figure at left is from Bolivia; the other two are from Peru. Llama at right wears a silver chain and bell. All are highly stylized and avoid detail. They illustrate the current mix of old and new in Latin-American carving.

Figs. 9 and 10. The Chinese are adept at elaborate and multi-level woodcarvings. These two antiques are typical. Fig. 9 is a drawer front with low-relief figures atop high-relief grounding, finished by lacquering and gilding. Fig. 10 is much more elaborate, a scene with pierced carving and in multiple planes, so foreground objects are undercut to clear the background. It was a cabinet panel several hundred years ago.

out the carvings in quantity—and most of the Seris went back to fishing and basketmaking. The story was much the same in Guatemala, Costa Rica and Honduras, where Indians make quite good carvings, and in Nicaragua, where all I saw were crude ones, obviously at least blanked on a bandsaw.

The reason for all this is simple. It's money. In countries where the economy is poor, a man who can carve can earn more than one who works in the fields, so carving is often considered to be a gift of God or of Allah. In very few areas of the world are there amateur carvers like most of us in the U.S.A.—the economy simply does not provide high wages, vacations, retirement benefits, and all the rest. Also, the educational level is not so high that the individual yearns to be cultured. I have talked to hundreds of carvers in so-called third world countries and can't recall one who carved for fun alone. Occasionally, I found one who had carved a unique piece to decorate his house or to give to a sweetheart, or as a toy for his child, but even those pieces could be bought. I remember a young Mexican Indian who sold me two Magi carved so recently that the blanco

wood was still exuding sap. (They molded during shipment back home!) He explained that he carved to feed his wife and new son, that the Lord had blessed him with a skill. Later that day, I saw him with his wife carrying the new son. He was coming from the market, and when he saw me, he excitedly came running up to show me a full market bag and a new broom—that's where my payment had gone.

Outside the U.S.A., carving is still a craft, with occasional art, creativity and originality, but is basically a way to earn money. I could go on, but let me make one last point now: In the United States, woodcarving is alive and growing rapidly, but largely as a hobby and/or a semi-professional vocation. We probably have more whittlers in this country today than we had in the first 200 years of its existence put together. Two societies have memberships totalling more than 60,000 and have more than 300 chapters or associated clubs. There are thousands of other whittlers and woodcarvers who belong to no organization, either because they prefer not to or are too isolated. My first book sold 20,000 copies in the years from 1936 to 1958, and has sold a quarter-million more as a paperback since 1962. Others have sold upwards of 50,000 in the past ten years—an indication of the tremendous surge in spare-time activities during the past two decades. We have early retirement, pensions, Social Security, and the urge to create something, with the funds to indulge ourselves. This is also true of Canada and England, the latter to a lesser extent.

"Whittling" is an Anglo-Saxon word, but is largely obsolete in England and Scotland, at least as applied to the working of wood. It has survived here in the U.S.A. longer probably because of our greater and more isolated farm population, as well as because of the interest retained by such groups as the Boy Scouts. Every man and boy had his pocketknife until relatively recent years, when—at least in urban areas—the possession of a knife became an automatic indication of hoodlumism. As has been said, "Americans can and will whittle." They still do—and more so than ever.

Many of the products of American whittling were primarily tricks to impress non-whittlers: fan, ball-in-a-cage, pliers, chain, whammydiddle. But many others were quite usable panels and figurines, the latter often depicting farm or wild animals and local "color." Practical objects like chip-carved boxes, pegs, tines, bows, toys for the children, weathervanes, windmills, "hex" signs, ship models and the like were produced as well. But most pieces were hand size, so the tradition of whittling things from a single piece of wood grew up

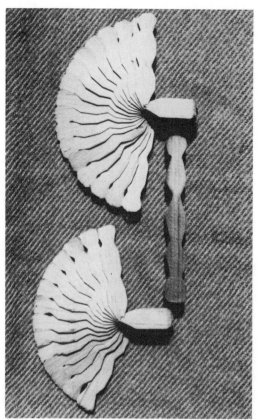

Fig. 11. The ball-in-a-cage and fan were standard beginner projects in whittling. Here are two simple fans and the blank for a double fan (split from both ends carefully to a stop in the middle). They are one-piece carvings and the trick in fan making is soft pine or basswood, soaked thoroughly before splitting is attempted. The pivot joint is a problem because the joint pins love to split off.

in contrast to the woodcarver's frequent assembly of elements like arms and legs on figures, or appliqué of stand-out parts of a panel.

Some unique whittling disappeared with the old tramp or hobo and his basic transportation, the railroad car. These men, often in return for a hot meal, or a night or two in a warm, dry hayloft, whittled pieces of packing boxes or cigar boxes rapidly into picture frames, whatnot boxes, comb boxes, and the like. These are now prized antiques, even though the hobo often didn't bother to pull off or cut away labels and stamping. He simply cut a series of stepped squares or rectangles, notched the edges, and glued the stack to form a squat pyramid. One, two, or three

pyramids would be nailed or glued to a drawer or box front. This is now grouped with "crown-of-thorns" carving as "tramp carving"—a misnomer for the thorny pieces.

Nowadays woodcarving, whether original or copy, is expensive by today's standards, and the fashion has been simplicity. Recently, however, between the urge to collect antiques and the rise of craft interests with added leisure time, woodcarving is coming back. And thousands of present or would-be woodcarvers are doing their own thing in their own way—with a full toolkit, with just a knife, or assisted by power tools. And most of them are amateurs.

Some of the more impatient workers in wood quickly adapted the hand grinder, the dental drill, files and rasps and other devices to speed up the preliminary shaping or the finishing. I know whittlers now who use power sanders, who sandblast or blowtorch in finishing for certain effects, and most whittlers now use bandsaws or scroll saws in rough shaping. Also, we have carved ivory, bone, soap, and more recently plastics, although not to the extent that this is done in Germany, Russia, Bali, Japan and China, for example. The isolated whittler anywhere in the world has always cut whatever was cuttable.

It has been my good fortune to be able to research many designs, techniques, and styles of woodcarving, and to experiment with most. In the process, I have collected many designs and have also developed my own in my chosen retirement business of carving what many pros wouldn't bother to attempt. Much of this would be in the general category of whittling or folk carving, but all of it has been fun. I would like to convey some of this to you. Included are hundreds of designs, many of them my own. The others include the best of such carving now being done here and abroad, and some older designs from my earlier books now out of print with new material to update them. My intention is to add new and different patterns to those available in my earlier books to help you build your carving ability while you are developing your knowledge, and, hopefully, an itch to design for yourself those carvings you yearn to make. I have particularly tried to select designs that are salable, because so many present-day carvers are what might be called semi-pros—they sell when the opportunity offers and take commissions when they can. I also hope to preserve for posterity the best designs, particularly from foreign countries now rapidly modernizing and forgetting inherited designs and skills. This is the same process the United States went through earlier this century, when mass production took over while the demand for such traditional carvings as cigar-store Indians, ship figureheads, and household carved objects and decorations declined.

The modern carver's world in the United States now is as much dominated by faddism as always. Some carvers restrict themselves to a few designs which they carve repeatedly. However, there are many hardy pioneers who continually seek something new and challenging to carve, or some interesting and different way of doing the carving, in the process of developing their own designs and techniques. It is to these explorers that this book is addressed.

E.J. Tangerman

Fig. 12 (opposite page). Whittling is a very old hobby, as these examples from a *Popular Mechanics Magazine* contest in the mid-Thirties prove. There were hundreds of whittled pieces entered, almost all in soft wood. Many chains can be seen, as well as a fan (bottom right) and a ball-in-a-cage (left center).

Part 1
Techniques and Design

1

Wood Never Surrenders

For the past 75 years, I have preferred wood to any other material and carving to any other avocation. I admire and respect wood, and am still impressed by what can be done with it (and shocked by what is sometimes done *to* it in the name of art). It is a warm and living material, and it conveys that warmth and life to its products in most instances. Since I wrote my first book, more than 50 years ago, I have tried to pass on to others my enthusiasm for wood and how satisfying working with it can be.

But, with all its virtues, wood is the most disobliging and refractory of common materials. Stone is cold and dead to carve and to touch. All the familiar metals are alike in that they can be hammered or poured into shape and will stay there as slaves to man. Not wood! It never ceases its efforts to get even. It warps, cracks, splits, develops knots and rotten spots just where they'll do the most damage. It dulls and breaks tools and shows grain and figure where they are least welcome. It never quite comes up to the carver's expectations. Even after completion, it will develop checks with changes of weather, invite insects and dry rot, and break when dusted. It changes color with time and rejects protective coverings. And any dust from its processing will penetrate the tightest barriers, including in some cases, the lungs of the carver if he isn't careful.

And what does Man do to wood? He cuts, chews, chars, warps, grinds, twists and otherwise tortures it. He expects super wood strength from thin sections, glues on pieces, inserts glass eyes, metal, other woods, and Lord knows what else. He daubs on paint and fillers, stains, bleaches—all to hide the wood itself. He crushes it in a vise or sticks screws into it, hammers and cuts it, and expects it to accept detail beyond its fibre capacity. And these undignified things are done in the name of art, craft, commerce, or just to pass the time.

No, don't talk to me of the romance between Man and wood! It's a battle, not a love affair, and never forget it! Relax your watchfulness for just a moment and the wood will turn or break your tool, split, break, or try some other trickery—it does not accept defeat or slavery gracefully. It will challenge you every time you try something new—and sometimes when you try to repeat something. You may win in the end, but you'll know you've been in a fight—trees may die, but wood never surrenders.

How can Man master wood? I've been seeking the answer to that question all my life, and I've carved all that time, but I still bow out when people ask how long it takes to develop real skill. I'm certain I shan't live long enough to achieve perfection, but I pray the Good Lord will let me keep on carving even after I'm dead. I've been learning all this time, and have been trying to pass it on, but there is always much more to learn and tell—hence this book.

Woodcarving, like most other arts,

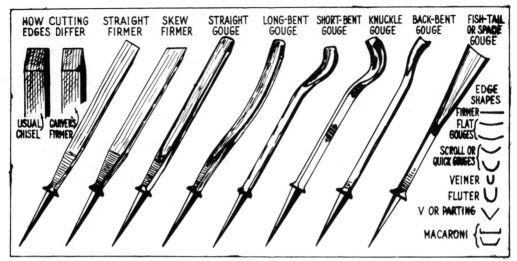

Fig. 1.1. Typical carving tool shapes and the cuts they make.

crafts, and games has a special vocabulary. Here are some of my definitions for terms used herein. *Whittling* is done with a single tool, usually a knife. *Woodcarving* uses many. It is common to distinguish between *chisels* as flat tools and *gouges* as ones with *sweep* or curvature, as in carpentering. Actually, the woodcarving chisel is lighter and thinner than that used by a carpenter, and is sharpened from both sides so that it won't dig in so readily, particularly if you swap hands. It is called a *firmer*. If the cutting edge is at an angle to the blade end, the tool is a *skew*. Gouges can range from ones with high *sweep* (long-arc curves)— meaning that they are almost flat—to ones that are U-shaped. Normal gouges may be distinguished by number or radius of sweep, depending upon source. You can get gouges in a wide range of sweeps. A gouge that is small in sweep and a half circle in cross-section is called a *veiner*, while a U-shaped one is a *fluter*. If a tool has a blade wider than the shank, it is called a *spade* or *fishtail*. If it is bent in the shank, it may be *long-bent*, *short-bent* (or even a *knuckle* if the arc of the shank bend is a half-circle). There are also tools which are *back-bent*—the cutting edge is behind the axis of the shank. A tool that has a radiused end (which removes the corners and lessens corner dig-ins) is called a *bull-nose*. There is also a *V-tool* or *parting tool*, with a V-shaped blade cutting on two sides simultaneously. If a tool is box-shaped and cuts on three sides, it is a *macaroni* and if the three sides are joined at the corners by small arcs, it is a *fluteroni*—you'll probably never use either. In the special traditional parlance of relief carving, *setting-in* is driving a tool vertically into the wood along an outline to sever the fibres previous to *grounding* or *bosting*—using a gouge to remove background wood up to the subject to be carved. *Modelling* is doing the actual shaping of the surface of the subject. Most other terms used herein are self-evident, I hope.

Selecting a wood to suit a design can be quite difficult unless you stick to the familiar soft woods such as basswood, white pine ("yellow" in England), and jelutong, which are favored for whittling. Red alder, buckeye, willow, and poplar are not much harder but can create finishing problems and have a greater tendency to split. The fruit and nut woods are hard, can have perverse grain, check in drying, and are difficult to carve, but they take beautiful finishes. In my opinion, they should be worked with chisels.

Among the foreign woods, the African woods are likely to prove hard, tend to split, and so on. Imbuya, or African walnut, is an exception. It is very like walnut but lighter and a bit easier to work. "Mahogany" is a loose term applied to many woods, ranging from the light-colored Honduras (now hard to find) through Cuban, Latin-American and African, to the Philippine. The latter includes a variety of woods, most tending to be coarse, and they can vary widely in weight and color. Most are difficult to cut clean and won't take detail. There are also associated "white mahoganies" such as primavera and luan or luanda, which, though coarse grained, finish to look just like mahogany.

I could go on endlessly, because I have gone out of my way to try various woods, not only for major carvings, but in mobiles with as many as twenty individual elements of different woods. Much can be done by selecting wood color, grain, and "figure" to suit the subject being depicted. Or it may be that the particular project calls for wood of unusual dimensions or unusual shape, in which case I use the best wood I have available regardless of relative carving difficulty. The alternative in some cases is to glue up commercially-available wood, a nuisance which can cause later trouble when flaws or knots suddenly appear well inside the surface, or adjacent grain structures are not compatible. Then there is always the possibility of running into an old bullet or a series of wormholes in the worst possible place. That has happened to me too.

There are several things you should know about wood in general. Knots and burls can cause trouble in carving unless you are skilled, but burls in particular can give very interesting carved effects, including figure and color. Dense woods tend to be harder than open-grained ones, but not always. Wide rings in oak and narrow rings in pine indicate greater hardness. Heartwood is harder and better colored than sapwood, and dry wood is harder than green or wet wood.

Some carvers prefer green wood (when there is no checking problem) and will occasionally keep the wood wet to ease carving—for example, on red alder and cottonwood. Weathering is important only with soft woods. The danger is usually decay—woods like red oak, red gum, apple, beech, elm, spruce, shortleaf pine and hemlock decay readily. White oak, slippery elm, black walnut, hickory, longleaf pine, tamarack and Douglas fir are medium-lived. Long-lived woods are cypress, redwood, red cedar, white cedar, Osage orange, catalpa, and locust. Fruitwoods in general do not last long if exposed to a combination of air and dampness and they are prone to insect attack. If a wood is subject to checking, it may be necessary to keep it damp during any protracted carving period, particularly if it is heartwood—in which case it may split later when it dries. Watch out for ash, apple, mesquite, and other woods in this category if your carving has any dimension. Some wood panels will warp in the sun if carved on one side: basswood, white pine, mahogany—even walnut.

Some woods impart taste or odor to foods, particularly to butter, so are not good for bowls, for example. If you rate ash, which imparts neither odor nor taste, as 100, soft maple is 84, hackberry 83, sycamore 80, beech 73, yellow poplar 71, soft elm 68, black gum 64, cottonwood and red gum 58. And if you're plagued with shavings or ruined pieces, the best firewoods are hickory, beech, hornbeam, locust, and heart pine. Oak, ash, birch, and maple are good. Spruce, fir, chestnut, hemlock, and sap pine are moderately good. White pine, alder, linden, cottonwood, basswood, and their ilk burn poorly. The facts, plus most of the accompanying table, are derived from studies by the U.S. Forestry Service, supplemented by observations by the author and two friends, Ken Thompson in Colorado and Hal McClure in North Carolina—which provides considerable range.

11	H
	M
	H
VH	
161	
H	
M	
79	
115	
H	
106	
102	
108	
200	
32	
H	
142	
35	
L	
VH	
H	
VH	

...light, ...t. The ...termine ...nd work-

ability numbers—the higher the harder. Heartwoods also tend to be hard to carve. "Checks" refers to tendency to check when drying.

Remarks	Grain	lb/cu ft	Work-ability	Hard-ness
rown		28	1	48
	VC	47	2	118
Grayish brown, pinkish		41	1	108
s. Light brown.	C	27	2	31
ny white, no visible grain	C	26	1	31
ecks. Shallow carving only.	C	45	2	96
ard. Visible yellow grain.	C	39	2	58
ark brown. Splits and cracks.	C		3	H
ft. Tan and cream mix.	C	25	1	31
dium hard. Like white walnut		27	1	40
t softer				
but colorful grain.	C	29	1	43
inkish	VC	29	1	48
scented, V red	VC	33	1	81
in, good finish	C	35	3	72
ayish brown and	O	30	1	50
od. Nice grain.	O	32	4	62
, varied	VC	80	4	VH
ite, sticky to cut	C	28	2	36
	C	32	2	52
nd difficult	VC	51	3	154
	O	34	2	59
lack and hard	VC	50	4	VH
lack and hard	VC	61	4	VH
light stripes	VC	50	4	VH
	VC	36	2	66
	C	52	H	H
e	O	36	3	11
red tinge. Not good	O	31	M	3
	VC	70	4	VH

Wood	Remarks	Grain	lb/cu ft	a
Gum, black & tupelo	Warps, twists		35	
Guayacan (Mexican)	Brown to green, striated	O	4	
Harewood (English sycamore)	V white, satiny	VC	40?	
Hemlock	Pale buff. Hard to carve.		33	3
Hickory, bigleaf	Stringy, light tan	O	48	3
Holly	Checks, V white	VC	40	4
Hornbeam, hop		O	50	4
Imbuya (African walnut)	Dark brown	C	35?	2
Ironwood, desert	V dark purple-brown	VC	80	2
Jacaranda (Brazil rosewood)		VC	53	4
Jelutong	Like white pine		25?	1
Larch	Red-brown, soft	O	36	2
Laurel, mountain		O	48	3
Lignum Vitae	Very hard. Dark brown	VC	80	4
Locust, black or yellow	Checks, medium brown	VC	48	3
Madroña	Warps, red-brown	C	46	4
Magnolia	Shallow carving only	O	?	1
Mahogany, African	Dark red-brown	O	42	2
Maple, red	Light red-brown	C	38	2
Maple, sugar	Light red-brown	C	44	2
Mesquite	Light yellow, insect attacks	C	?	2
Myrtle	Grayed brown and gray	C	39	2
Oak, black	Checks	C	43	3
Oak, red	Checks coarser, splinters	C	44	2
Osage orange	Brown and yellow stripes. Splits	VC	53	4
Paradise tree (paulownia)	Nice grain		24	1
Pear	Tawny yellow. Checks. Twisty	C	?	2
Pecan	Checks	C	47	3
Pine, white	V soft, yellow tinge	C	25	1
Pine, yellow	Splits, checks, light brown pattern	C	28	2
Pink Ivory	Reddish pink	VC	?	H
Poplar, yellow	Yellowish white, soft, splits	C	28	L
Purpleheart	Lavender to dark purple	VC	H	3

Fig. 1.2. This piece of Virginia cedar, found in an Ohio marl pit, is one of the oldest pieces of wood in the world. Carbon dating shows it to be 8,500 years old, plus or minus 500 years.

WOOD CHARACTERISTICS—continued

Wood	Remarks	Grain	lb/cu ft	Work-ability	Hard-ness
Redwood (sequoia)	Red to deep red, hard to carve	O	30	1	59
Rhododendron	Bush	C	40	2	104
Rosewood	Many varieties and colors	C	?	3	VH
Sandalwood	Scented, creamy white	C	M	2	M
Sassafras	Checks, tan, striated		32	1	60
Satinwood	Satiny translucence and figure	C	64	3	H
Sourwood	Greyish-white		38	1	40
Spruce	Resinous	C	28	2	40
Sumac	Pithy. Good withes		33	2	64
Sycamore	Checks	VC	35	3	64
Teak	Red-brown	VC	36	2	M
Vermilion	Red, grain figure	VC	?	3	H
Walnut, black	Checks. Chocolate brown	C	39	2	88
Willow, black	Checks and splits—withes	O	26	2	35
Willow, red	Similar, but carves better	O	25	2	M
Witch Hazel	Flexible	VC	43	2	107
Yew	Flexible	VC	44	1	33
Zebrawood	Striated, brown and tan, splits	O	?	3	H

2

Seven Easy Whittlings

Domestic birds and animals are traditional whittling subjects, readily carved by the beginner, at least in simpler designs like these. Further, these designs from Thailand are a bit different from our familiar ones and add an interesting fillip—a "secret" compartment in the body. This was perhaps originally cut in for prayers to be inserted, as in the dragon duck of Bali, but are now much more useful as temporary hiding places for rings and small jewelry. (The design can of course be enlarged to take larger pieces.) In most of these examples, the hole is simply drilled in, then squared up and a dovetail slide added in a connecting slot. The rooster, however, separates at mid-body to provide a larger and more elaborately carved chamber, and one frog has a semi-concealed trapdoor in its back.

All of these designs are carved in soft wood and are stained dark, but could readily be painted or carved in harder woods. And the compartments are of course not obligatory if you have no rings to hide. Finish can range from almost utter plainness to elaborate texturing, although none of these pieces is overdone. A stylized suggestion of feathers is created in the ducks by parallel cuts with a small gouge to stoplines cut with a knife or firmer, and on one duck these cuts have been filled with white pigment, apparently after staining. Wing shapes are also outlined with a V-tool and eyes are inserted glass beads. The small frog and turtle have no secret compartments, although they could have, but the larger frog is quite a good design, carefully executed, with a clever trapdoor arrangement. The rooster is also more elaborate than the others because of its twisted head and nicely hollowed fanned tail.

Fig. 2.1. Small turtle and frog are solid figures, but could also have secret compartments with base slides.

Figs. 2.2 and 2.3 (above). Heavy-beaked rooster and trick-tailed frog both have secret compartments for jewelry. Each is about 4-in. (102-mm) long.

Figs. 2.4 and 2.5 (below). Small ducks 1- to 2-in. (25- to 51-mm) long have base slides for concealing rings. They probably originally carried prayers in Thailand.

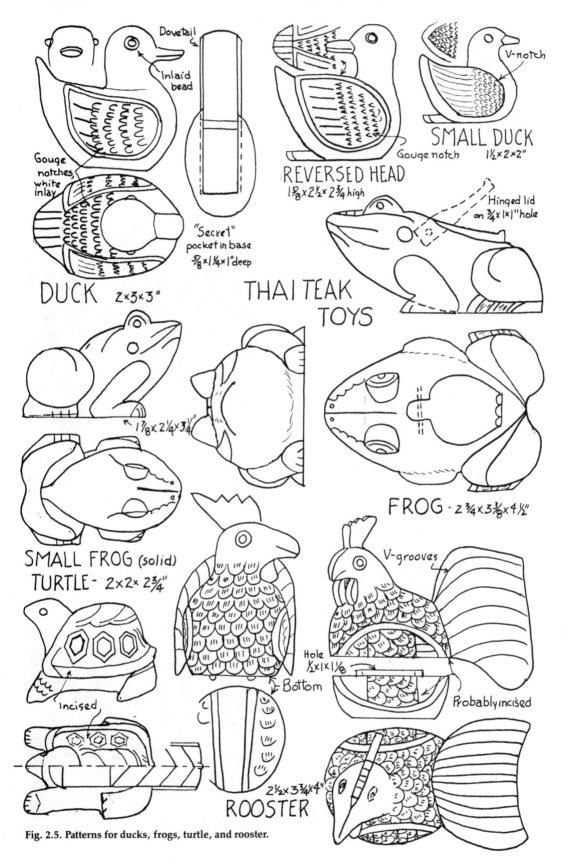

Dovetail

Inlaid bead

Gouge notches white inlay

"Secret" pocket in base
$5/8 \times 1 1/4 \times 1$" deep

DUCK $2 \times 3 \times 3$"

REVERSED HEAD
$1 5/8 \times 2 1/2 \times 2 3/4$ high

Gouge notch

V-notch

SMALL DUCK $1 1/2 \times 2 \times 2$"

Hinged lid on $3/4 \times 1 \times 1$" hole

THAI TEAK TOYS

FROG - $2 3/4 \times 3 3/8 \times 4 1/2$"

$\leftarrow 1 7/8 \times 2 1/4 \times 3 1/4$"

SMALL FROG (solid)

TURTLE - $2 \times 2 \times 2 3/4$"

Incised

Bottom

V-grooves

Hole
$1/2 \times 1 \times 1 1/8$

Probably incised

$2 1/2 \times 3 3/4 \times 4$"

ROOSTER

Fig. 2.5. Patterns for ducks, frogs, turtle, and rooster.

3

Design to Fit the Wood

The carpenter and the cabinetmaker begin with processed wood and tend to discard any sections which might offer a challenge, or to conquer such a problem as a knot by veneering the piece. Not so for the carver, who even in more-predictable relief carving must contend with knots, soft spots and vagrant grain. In time, this sort of flaw becomes a challenge.

In the harder woods such as walnut and cherry, it is almost inevitable that a carver will encounter problems with unpredictable grain unless he selects his wood very carefully and is thereafter blessed with luck. I have worked so much walnut over so many years that I *assume* I'll encounter trouble at some point. In fact, I have one client who has bought three walnut carvings from me because she is fond of knots! And in this book I describe a cherry panel with a dragon wagon that was hailed by this client because the wood contained wavy grain and bird's-eye areas.

Thus, I should like to suggest that at times it is advisable to yield to the wood and see if it doesn't suggest its own design, either by its shape or the so-called flaws in it. Here are two carvings in cedar, both in-the-round, that I think may serve as good examples. In both cases, the wood told me what to do, and I did it—to our mutual benefit. There were no drawings or patterns for either—the pattern developed as I carved.

Cedar has never impressed me particularly as a carving wood; it tends to be soft, likes to split, and has an odor and

Fig. 3.1. The original cedar log had three knots that were strategically placed for a teddy bear but nothing but trouble for the planned Indian bust.

color that some people find objectionable. I have carved it when I was in a hurry, and have made both in-the-round and panel carvings of it, so I accepted the offer of a friend who had just cut down a small cedar to take a couple of lengths. I'd seen some first-class Indian busts carved in cedar and thought I'd like to try one.

So I dutifully selected the slimmer of the two pieces and mounted it with a carver's screw. I skinned off the outer bark and began to round the top for the head. As I rotated the piece, I saw three knots where branches had been cut away long since (see

Fig. 3.2. The head was designed around the topmost knot and cutting begun with a 1¼-in. (32-mm) carpenter's gouge.

Fig. 3.3. It was obvious that upper arms had to be hanging straight down—that's where the wood was, and it was already evident that growth wood could help by putting color in the right places.

Fig. 3.1), and they made such an indelible picture of a teddy bear that my Indian bust idea lost its glamour. One of the knots was obviously a nose and the two side by side were feet so the Indian head never really had a chance. A teddy bear it became, and I'm glad, because the white growth wood provided a nose and belly that contrasted with the red of the rest. Besides, it sold at once to a friend who saw my photo of it, and it took far less time than the bust would have.

Somewhat ashamed of myself, however, I prepared the second piece, only to realize that it was deeply fissured and oval in cross-section, hence not very suitable for a bust either. It did, however, suggest a dragon, with coils matching the contours of the cross-section. So I carved the dragon, and gave her soulful eyes to make her a lady. Again the growth wood worked in my favor, although a couple of spots had to be tinted to match the prevailing red base color. I also added a forked tongue and tinted it to match. The piece did *not* elicit hosannas at home, but it was the first piece sold in my 1986 one-man show—and

was bought by the chairwoman of the show, who has a doctorate in art.

These two examples may help you get over the "What shall I carve?" syndrome. A section of plank or a block of squared-up wood are unlikely to give any carver much in the way of an idea, but a section of tree, a random piece of driftwood, or even a slab from a tree will do so in many cases. (It may not do so at once, but leave the piece out where you can see it regularly and an inspiration is almost certain to come.) And many of these pieces of wood will be relatively soft, therefore faster carving, so there's no great loss if you give it up in the process.

As to details of the carving: No pattern is really necessary for either of these two examples, because they conform to a particular piece. I am, however, providing one pattern as a point of departure for your design on a similarly shaped block. It will also help, if you have a particular hunch about a piece, to do a little research on the subject; you'll be surprised at what you find in your local library and in various woodcarving books, to say nothing of tra-

Fig. 3.4. As final shaping began, I shifted to a 1-in. (25-mm) firmer and ½-in. (13-mm) flat and deep gouges, with ⅛- and ¼-in. (3- and 7-mm) firmers for details. The surfaces were intentionally left with gouge marks to suggest heavy pelt, and the base was left with only slight cleaning off of stringy bark.

Fig. 3.5. The back was left essentially simple and straight, with little attempt to modify growth-wood areas, but the front was retouched slightly where needed. Note the toes on hind legs. Eyes and nose tip were darkened for effect.

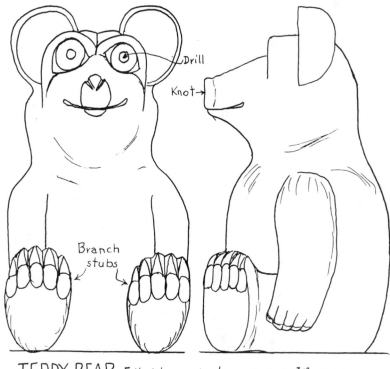

TEDDY BEAR—Fitted to a cedar log. 9×9×15¾" No color

Fig. 3.6. Pattern for teddy bear.

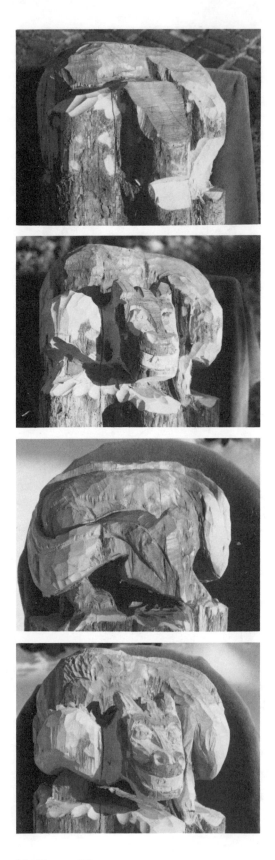

Fig. 3.7. This piece of cedar was oval and had deep crevices so was unsuitable for a bust, while one projecting rib made a natural head shape. Here the head has been separated and a curl of the body is delineated above it.

Fig. 3.8. The major problem is to figure out the coils of the body and work around them. Here the head and neck have been worked out on the front.

Fig. 3.9. Here is the forked tail outlined in back. Note that I decided on four legs to be visible and tunnelled under the body to establish them.

Fig. 3.10. The neck had to have an inward wave because of log conformation, and it was also given a vertical wave for interest.

Fig. 3.11. The tail is being developed.

Fig. 3.12. Here the shaping is practically complete. Note the standup back ridge, which is notched with saw and firmer. Eye pupils are drilled holes and mouth is being sawed open between the teeth to take the tongue, a separate piece.

Fig. 3.13 (above). Again, the base is left largely unchanged except for loose bark. On this figure, however, it was necessary to touch up some areas of growth wood to darken them for the body. Face is left white, but eyes and nose are detailed and tinted. Separate tongue is tinted red also.

Fig. 3.14 (below). This was my original intention—an 11-in. (219-mm) Indian bust in cedar. This one was carved by George Foral of Omaha, Nebraska, at the summer school at Deane College staged by a NWCA chapter there, where many similar busts are carved annually.

ditional pottery, stone figures, calendars, posters, and other illustrations. You need a fairly clear picture in your mind of the subject before you begin; otherwise you'll cut away wood that you will need later.

Pieces like these can be carved with full-sized tools. I used a 1-in. medium-sweep gouge for much of the roughing, and did much of the smoothing with a 2½-in. flat gouge, with a heavy mallet. Detailing takes smaller and lighter tools, but they can still be full-size if you have them. I'm talking of a ½-in. (13-mm) wide firmer and gouges of several different sweeps, plus V-tool and smaller gouges. And for this sort of caricature, don't waste a lot of time sanding and smoothing; it looks better left somewhat rough—unless it's something that *must* be smooth like a seal, a nude, or even that carefully detailed Indian bust I never got to.

4

Design to Fit Odd Shapes

Potential carving blocks need not be rectangular. In fact they often are more challenging and interesting if they are not. I've written several times about the many Balinese carvings with roughly triangular or irregularly oval bases done because that was the shape of the available wood. By coincidence, after a commission I had two triangular shafts of walnut to design for that were 5 × 5 × 7-in. (127 × 127 × 178 mm) and 24 in. (610 mm) long.

I decided to do two quite different carvings, one an in-the-round and the other a low-relief pierced carving in the Balinese style. Because of the length of the pieces available, the in-the-round section sug-

gested a dragon with splayed feet and a curving tail, but no wings unless I were to add them later. I decided to leave the 7-in. (178-mm) side ½ in. (13 mm) thick as a base. The dragon turned out to be a relatively simple carving, which was my objective, except for the matter of holding it so that regular large tools and a medium-weight mallet could be used to get rid of waste wood rapidly. The problem was how to hold the piece by some temporary device. The answer was a pine block about

Fig. 4.1. Left: Step 1—The design is sketched on both upper faces, and cutting begun. Center: Step 2—General form of the body is worked out and hollowing begun. Right: Step 3—Spinal ridge and feet are detailed and body shaped.

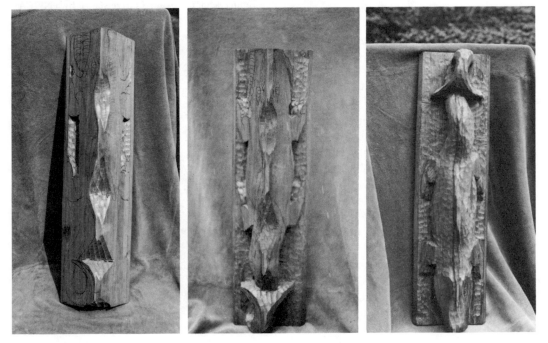

Fig. 4.2. Step 4—Hollowing under tail is done and loop of tail drilled and shaped.

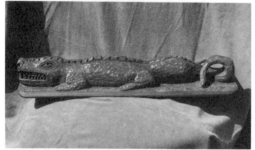

Fig. 4.3. Step 5—Head is shaped, including drilling around teeth and shaping them.

¾ × 3 × 4 in. (19 × 76 × 101 mm) with a vee notch cut across it. This fitted over the center ridge of the triangle and made it possible to hold the piece in a standard carpenter's vise, and to adjust the angle readily. Because the piece was a triangle, the upper 5-in. (127-mm) sides could be worked on with ease; most of the time I was sitting down. Having carved a number of dragons, I knew the problems in depicting scales, so I decided to simulate them by small scallops with a flat gouge, and to make the back ridge-spines by drilling through at ½- to 1-in. (13- to 25-mm) inter-

vals at the base of the spine and sawing down vertically with coping saw cuts to meet each hole. The sloping cuts could be done with a firmer. While this method requires knife or rasp smoothing to eliminate saw marks, it is much faster than normal chisel cutting because of the problems of splitting off the pointed edge of each tooth. (My spine design is a sort of circular-saw tooth shape, but a triangular shape will work just as well—then both cuts can be sawed.)

Obviously, a carving such as this can be expedited also by drilling through at suitable places around the tail and between the teeth in the open jaw. (The open jaw makes it unnecessary to separate the underjaw from the base.) Because small drills sometimes take odd directions in drilling, the holes between teeth were drilled in only to slightly past center from each side and the front, and the rest of the wood was removed with a ⅛-in. (3-mm) firmer and V-tool. Much of the rest of the carving, including the scales, was one with a 1-in. (25-mm) flat gouge.

I should mention that this design could be made at least as effectively without the integral base, except for the problems of holding it while carving. Elimination of the base would add ½ in. (13 mm) to the height of the figure itself and allow more freedom for the feet, so they could extend below the belly. Also, overall length could be de-

Fig. 4.4. Step 6—In final form—base is scalloped, horns added, spine notched.

creased to allow space at the front for a projecting tongue—if your dragons must have tongues. Or a tongue can be added just as I added the triple horns later. My horns are of holly, which gives an ivory-like look and resists breakage from accidental bumping. (The piece made four airplane-luggage trips without damage.)

Carving the body itself is routine. Most portions are massive, so cutting can be rapid. Details around the face and tail-tip require smaller tools, but even there the fact that the tail is secured to the base makes the likelihood of splitting small.

The pierced low-relief carving is, in contrast, much more demanding as a project, because it is relatively easy to crack carved portions in the process of hollowing the interior, and piercing with chisels is certain to cause some splitting out of inside wood if the interior is hollowed first. Also, because of the 24-in. (610-mm) length of the piece, it is practically impossible to hollow out the interior with conventional tools from the ends alone. It is, of course, possible to make the triangular shape as separate flat carvings and assemble them, before or after carving. This would certainly be no more difficult to carve than the piece I had, consisting as it did of various pieces of walnut glued together, so that grain had a habit of changing as I carved across a glued joint and knots appeared in unexpected places. Obviously, there are a number of ways to do such a piece; I can simply tell you of my experience in using up what might be called scrap.

The clamping method for the block worked out as well for the pierced carving as it did for the dragon, with reasonable care, of course. I started by carving one end in the desired low-relief pattern. I drilled in at areas to be pierced, being careful not to drill so deeply that I affected the opposite face. Essentially, I started with perhaps 3 in. (76 mm) of low-relief carving, with the piercing almost 1 in. (25 mm) deep. My design was haphazard, drawn in just ahead of where I was carving, and incorporated the vines connecting objects, similar to what I'd seen in Balinese hollow

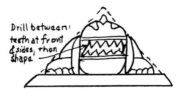

Fitted to a triangular walnut section roughly 7x5x5x24"

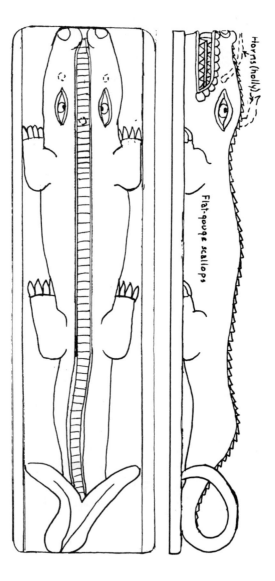

Fig. 4.5. Patterns for dragon.

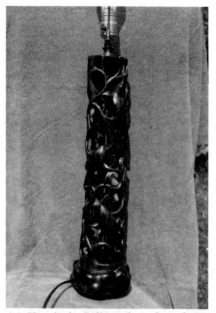

Fig. 4.6. Here is the Balinese lamp base that caused all the trouble. Note the delicacy of its haphazard "design as you carve." It is a 3½ in. (82.5 mm) cylinder 18½ in. (470 mm) long, with 5-in. (127-mm) base integral.

carvings like the lamp base pictured. (The lamp base was of macassar ebony, with walls about ¼-in. [6-mm] thick. Because mine was to be a wall plaque, I had already decided not to carve the 7 in. [178 mm] back.)

I soon realized that I had an anomalous situation. The pierced carving should be done with small tools to guard against cracking, but hogging out the interior wood, even with drilling at all possible points, was a job for heavy cutting. My thought had been that the solid back would be supportive, but I soon realized that I wouldn't want the back eventually anyhow, because it would not permit light or wall color to pass through and thus highlight the pierced portions. Further, as I worked in, I found that it was almost essential to be able to work from the back to clear out the central wood. So I compromised by carving out much of the back but leaving spaced cross straps so I could use my clamping block without risk of splitting the piece. (Obviously, in the early stages, the vise can always grip over solid wood in a piece like this, but at about the halfway

Fig. 4.7. Step 1—Initial carving is easy, because hollowing can be done from the end.

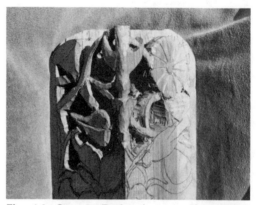

Fig. 4.8. Step 2—Design just precedes carving. Forms are simple, modelling minimal. Design along the rib is tricky.

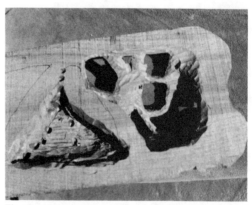

Fig. 4.9. Step 3—To handle the hollowing, the back is cut out, leaving reinforcing bars.

Fig. 4.10. Step 4—Motifs are placed haphazardly, but supported by connecting vines.

Fig. 4.11. Step 5—Drilling around designs must be done carefully, but expedites work.

Fig. 4.12. Step 6—The final end is the most difficult—it must work out sensibly and the whole triangle is now somewhat fragile. Note wood change in color near base.

mark, it is easier to begin clamping over finished portions.) Also, I found that no matter how carefully I carved, the walnut tended to split out inside if I removed the core first, and removing the core later required a good deal more piercing. I compromised by working both ways, but left a wall about ¾ in. (19 mm) thick for carving, then going back and thinning the wall when the carving was complete. The final wall is about ½-in. (13-mm) thick.

I continued the process of designing as I went, putting in stylized bird and flower units connected by vines, and being particularly careful on the front or top edge where the two carved sides joined. Even so, after a short time, I heard a rattle rather than a clean sound when the mallet hit— an indication that a crack had formed somewhere at the finished end. This was extremely difficult to locate because the carved section stayed tight, so the edges of the crack were not visible. I found that by careful tapping on each design in turn, I could locate the crack by a difference in the sound of the rattle; it was more pronounced at the crack point.

Repairs were made with Elmer's® glue thinned with water and carving proceeded, only to have the ominous sound recur a short time later. Probing showed the original crack to be sound, so another bit of detective work was required. After a couple of experiences like this, I began to realize that my heavy cutting of the interior was creating whip and vibration on the open end, and this was great enough to cause a crack. The solution was to clamp the carved end rather than the solid one, thus damping the vibration, and to be a bit less aggressive in hogging out the interior. (The open cuts through the back left only four or five straps about 1 in. [25 mm] wide to hold the shape against clamping pressure. These were eventually removed, except for the two at the ends of the piece.)

This sounds as though the carving is extremely difficult, but it isn't really—it just requires painstaking care and tools of reasonable size. The heavy ones that can be used on a solid piece are too heavy for this

Fig. 4.13. Step 7 (above)—Once carving is complete, these reinforcing bars will be removed, leaving straps only at the ends.

Fig. 4.14 (below). Patterns for pierced carving.

job—an indication of why so many Balinese carvers have tools only about ⅜ in. (9 mm) wide at most. A piece such as this is unique among present-day carvings, and will make a lovely wall hanging or lamp shield. The shape need not be triangular, of course; it can be multi-sided, cylindrical, or what-have-you. I am still cowed, however, when I look at that lamp base (Fig. 4.6). Base and top are integral, so the carver couldn't have bored through end to end. Inside walls are smooth and outside carving is flawless. Ironically, I

bought the piece for about $10 American— but that was 15 years ago. Today, one doesn't even see pieces like this in Bali.

For the pierced panel, my tools were: ½-in. (13-mm) V-tool; (30°), ⅝-in. (16-mm) and ⅜-in. (10-mm) flat gouges; ⅜-in. (10-mm) spade firmer; ⅛-in. (3-mm) firmer; and a knife. For the dragon, I added a ¼-in. (6-mm) flat gouge and a ⅛-in. (3-mm) 45° V-tool, both long-bent types. In general, for the pierced piece, short tools proved to be unhandy except for surface modelling.

Fig. 4.15. The pierced carving makes a beautiful wall hanging or lamp sconce.

5

Remember Point of View

Are you dealing with a carving likely to be displayed well above or below eye level? Carvers who make boat counters, signs, and weather vanes, and stone sculptors who decorate pediments or statuary, have long had a common problem—that of point of view. The observer stands well above or well below the carving, rather than facing it directly. I have known of cases in which a carver had to redo portions of his work to make it understandable (or readable in the case of lettering). I have found it advisable to deepen relief considerably if a panel is to be displayed well above eye level, and have on occasion had to modify a design because shadows caused problems. The difficulties are not limited to relief carvings, however; they can occur with in-the-round carvings as well.

Is the wood very light in color—like holly or maple, or very dark, like walnut? Will it be displayed in glaring or diffused light? For a light wood, it is advisable to put it in indirect light; for a dark wood, to increase the illumination. Also, lines should probably be carved in both cases deeper than usual and the carving should be "antiqued" by adding a darkening tint to lines and background to make them contrast with the main body of the carving. Or you may want to tilt the work slightly to change the effect of the lighting. I did that with a large panel that was to hide the fireplace opening in summer (it's called a fireboard)—I tilted it backward about 15° so viewers didn't have to stoop to examine it.

Fig. 5.1. A 16-in. (406-mm) bear in cherry is designed to be displayed on the floor, looking up appealingly at viewers. He has flat-gouge marks to suggest a cub's rough pelt and to show that he is hand-carved, not a casting.

Many things can be done to fit a carving to a desired environment. An obvious one is to select a proper pose. The bear cub is a good example. In essence, he is just a begging cub. A hand-size carving would be suitable anywhere, but a larger one is much improved by being below the line of sight, so the cub really appears to be begging. It makes an excellent doorstop, for example, as would a squatting dog or cat. A contrasting possibility is a cat designed to be shown on a high shelf—I carved several of these with tails hanging below the shelf edge. Birds with long hanging tails, like macaws, parrots and quetzals, can be similarly posed and break the monotony of figures "all in a row."

The bear has been popular with my students, so I provide patterns for him. My larger one was from a 9-in. (23-cm) long cherry log about 16 in. (40 cm) long. Carving was free-hand—no preliminary sawing—because of the dimensions and bulk of the design. Roughing was done with a 1-in. (25-mm) carpenter's gouge, finishing with woodcarving gouges from a ⅛-in. (3-mm) fluter for details like the eyes, to a ¾-in. (20-mm) medium-sweep one for the texturing. Pelt surfaces were not laboriously lined, but the rough coat was suggested by leaving shallow gouge marks. A V-tool was necessary for claws, mouth, and nostril detailing. Holes were drilled between the legs, then waste wood was chiselled out. A slightly darker stain (walnut) was applied to make nose tip and eye pupils stand out. (Note that in the hand-size version, the cub is a bit heftier and his legs are more widely spaced—a function of available wood.)

The lack of detailed hair on the cub brings up another point: Many carvers forget that details begin to disappear at a very short distance. They insist upon putting in hair on animals, eye corners, nail heads in siding, and much more—all of which serve no purpose if the carving is not going to be examined minutely. In essence: To make a brick chimney, it is not essential to carve every brick, nor is it meaningful to carve every shingle on a roof. Go and look at a roof or a chimney and you'll see that a few bricks or shingles will suggest the detail, and you'll find that too much detail makes a carving *less* attractive rather than more so. This is one of the few cases in which less work gives a better result.

Fig. 5.2. A smaller version of the begging cub is in pine, smooth-finished so he will be picked up and caressed. Note that he has a wider stance because the wood permitted it, and is slightly stockier as well. He is about 4 in. (102 mm) tall. The patterns show the wider stance. This piece is Swiss.

Fig. 5.3. Patterns for bear cub.

6

How to Carve a Portrait

Perhaps you can carve portrait faces easily; I can't. So when I was asked to carve a statuette by someone I couldn't really refuse, I admitted my weakness, particularly because the request was for a portrait of a 2-year-old boy. I learned long ago that carving the head of a child is particularly difficult, both because proportions keep changing as they grow, and because children's faces have no lines that identify them as adults' do. One can subtly emphasize outstanding ears, a noticeably pug nose or unusual eyes, but beyond that it is pure luck as far as I am concerned.

However, having no choice, I undertook the commission. I decided I'd carve in a very white wood. I had a section of holly trunk 3 × 3 × 6½ in. (76 × 76 × 315 mm) that seemed to fill the bill—it would take any requisite detail and could be whittled in a pinch—something that might be difficult with a larger block. Besides, I had several excellent photographs of the child in about the required size.

The carving procedure is detailed in the step-by-step photographs. As can be seen, I used a saw when possible (holly is *hard*)—once to my own disadvantage when I cut too deeply in the front (see Step 5), which made a good deal of later adjustment necessary. I chose to carve the head practically to completion before I undertook the rest of the body; I've learned that a very successful body carving can be ruined by a bad job on the head at the end. Also, I strove for a pose that would not be rigid, that would suggest some of the con-

Fig. 6.1. Step 1—Front and side sketches were drawn on flattened areas of the piece, and rough sawing done, outlines sawed away being replaced immediately.

Fig. 6.2. Step 2—The head was blocked out and roughed, taking care to maintain tilt and twist as well as leaving wood for ears, which were prominent.

Fig. 6.3. Step 3—The head itself was roughed in, because a portrait is almost entirely dependent upon the success of head carving. The rest is easy.

Fig. 6.4. Step 4—To attain the correct back-of-head shape, it is advisable to block in the back, particularly because of the body twist. Note neck muscles.

Fig. 6.5. Step 5—Here the head pose is quite visible, as well as the error in sawing too deeply just below the knee. Arms and shoulders are being shaped.

Fig. 6.6. Step 6—The legs are blocked in, position of the right leg being shifted from original plan. Hands are rough-formed, as well as hassock.

Fig. 6.7. Step 7—Note the dog under the right arm which also hides the right kneecap. Hands are now shaped and overall delineated. Sawdust hair attempted.

Fig. 6.8. Step 8—Hassock stitching is suggested and back completed. Foot is completed as well. Base is rounded to suggest original branch.

stant motion that is typical of children of that age, so the head was both tipped and turned, the legs and arms were in natural but difficult carving positions, the boy was to be seated on a hassock which in turn would be on a circular base showing the original shape of the wood. To accommodate the tilt in the torso, which raised the right arm, I decided to place a dog toy under that arm, and to pull the right leg up so it almost crossed the left knee, thus providing a resting place for the left hand. I had originally had the left leg down and the right hanging near it. This change in design, undertaken after original layout, projected the right foot into the unwise front sawing I'd do (Step 5), so I had to patch on a portion for the foot. This left a line that I couldn't eradicate because of the light color of the wood and the darker glue, so I had to add a moccasin sole finally (Step 7). However, I left a small and very black knot on the left knee as a "beauty mark."

I tried using a coating of glue with sawdust to simulate the sparse hair of a youngster, but that was simply no good.

Fig. 6.9. Step 9—The completed figure. Note moccasin on left foot, knot at left knee, added sole on right foot, hair change, careful hand detailing.

The ultimate solution was to put in a few suggestive hairlines and tint the hair slightly. Incidentally, the ears on this figure are very prominent, so must be carefully carved. The same goes for the hands.

Fig. 6.10. Pattern for 2-year-old boy.

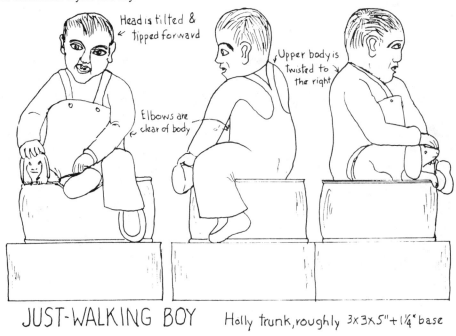

Head is tilted & tipped forward

Elbows are clear of body

Upper body is twisted to the right

JUST-WALKING BOY   Holly trunk, roughly 3×3×5" + 1¼" base

7

You *Can* Carve Miniatures

Painters and sculptors have known for a very long time that a client can readily be much more impressed by size than by content. Look at much of today's output for confirmation; it doesn't have to be really good if it is heroic (which in this context doesn't mean brave, but simply bigger than life). However, through the same period, a lesser number of really skilled artists and artisans have been making miniatures—witness the Fabergé eggs made for the Czar, or some of the exquisite ivory carvings made for emperors both in Europe and in Asia. Most miniature carving these days is done in Asia, but some is done in the American Southeast by Cherokee stone carvers and some on the West Coast by Indians like the Navajo, Hopi, Zuni, Haida, and Tlingit. Most of the Indian carvings are in stone, but can serve as patterns for larger woodcarvings, or for same-size designs in woods like holly and ebony that will take and hold detail.

I have been interested in miniatures ever since I can remember, and now have an extensive collection of miniatures in many materials. A high percentage of these are turtles and frogs less than an inch (25 mm) long in semi-precious stones that were made in Mexico. A couple of dozen fish, dogs, and what-have-you are from Rio, again made by Indians; as many others are Cherokee pieces in red pipestone and black steatite. Among the latter are a number of pieces that I call "mystic" for want of a better term; they often have a number of images on one piece, each bleeding into another, or becoming an-

Fig. 7.1. Four challenging pieces, a basswood gnome (painted) by George Foral of Omaha, two holly figures of mine, and a Chinese antique masterpiece with extreme detail, once painted and gilded.

Fig. 7.2. The 12 years which succeed one another in China have colorful names. These tiny figures in serpentine symbolize them. Each is quite well finished—and they're the size shown here.

Fig. 7.3. Charlie Reed, Cherokee, carved these two miniature statuettes, the first a seated lady with a dog in her arms, the other a bent old lady leaning on her stick, with a bag over her shoulder. I have a number of his pieces, even smaller than these and just as detailed, including a tiny dog or two less than ¼ in. (6 mm) tall.

Fig. 7.4. Charlie Reed also carved these figures in red pipestone, a man crawling over a log with left arm bent and left leg in the air, a sturdy squatting bear, and a seated Indian chief. I got the crawling figure home safely, but lost the chief's standing eagle feather—about half as tall as he is. Pipestone is fragile.

Fig. 7.5. These red pipestone figures are typical Cherokee. The bear is seated on a dime, and the longer figure has nine different subjects carved on it!

Fig. 7.6. A Cherokee had fun carving this hatted turtle in red pipestone. He is standing on a dime.

Fig. 7.7. Mexico is the source of these figures carved in bone, both having to do with the Day of the Dead, a religious holiday there. The figure at left is a skeleton with six smaller skeletons crawling over it, the smaller one is a family portrait, the male skeleton (I think) standing behind his seated wife with a child at her feet—all skeletons. The family is 1 in. (25 mm) tall, the group is 1¼ in. (31 mm) tall.

Fig. 7.8. China is the source of this monkey group in soapstone, very intricate and less than 4 in. (100 mm) tall. This is a common "tourist piece," but fun.

Figs. 7.9 and 7.10. Northwest Coast Indians carve miniature animals like these, shown here twice actual size. Both are in rhodonite, a pinky-red stone.

Fig. 7.11. Hematite, an iron ore, yields brilliant black figures. These two are from British Columbia and carved by Indians. They are double actual size.

other when inverted. One, for example, has about eight or nine eagle heads that I've found, and there may be others. One that I didn't buy in time was of a six-legged turtle about an inch (25 mm) long; the carver explained it by his title for it: "Rough Road."

My own efforts at miniaturizing pale beside any of these, but I have done a lot of it in the process of making models, usually in wood, such as men ¾-in. (16-mm) tall and the like. I know Mexican jewelers who have made patterns of dancers about that size in pochotlé bark, a reddish wood that is also carved by Mexican Indians into miniature scenes. The wood is relatively soft but will hold detail, so can be used for patterns that will be cast into gold or silver pendants. The same Indians, by the way, also make miniature figures in clay of dancers, rooms, dishes, and animals playing instruments, finishing them with gay painting; tourists gobble them up. I can't forbear mentioning here the dressed fleas that used to be sold along the Border for a dime or a quarter. Dead fleas were mounted as heads for tiny figures made of cloth—the whole in a ¼ in. (6 mm) box. And I have also seen figures on top of matchsticks of Don Quixote on his nag Rosinante, and Sancho Panza on a donkey. These are wood about ¼-in. (6-mm) tall, and the owner keeps them in her safe.

But back to carving miniatures: The principal needs are a small knife and a pair of eyes, both very sharp, plus hands that are steady and predictable. Figures can be carved on the end of a stick of suitable diameter so as to provide a grip, then separated later if you dare. It is important, at least initially, to use designs that do not involve long projections. Keep a man's hands at his sides; avoid single feathers, thin legs (particularly across grain) and the like. (They can be carved, but preferably in such materials as cherry pits or ivory.) I remember seeing a cherry pit carved into a caricature of Richard Nixon at a show in Ohio, and owned one from Ecuador that carried the bust of a general. And I own three or four little red seeds from India that

Fig. 7.12. Southwestern American Indians carve many miniatures also: Witness this skunk, here about twice actual size. It is actually a laminate of black stone surrounding a central white stripe, and was carved by a Navajo.

Fig. 7.13. Turquoise is the material of this Navajo big-horn sheep, one of two damaged figures I bought and repaired with turquoise from the same source. Here he is about 1½ times actual size, and the lower half of the horn is mine.

Fig. 7.14. Turquoise wolverine (?) is a Navaho fetish from Santa Fe.

Fig. 7.15 Hematite, a shiny black mineral, is apparently the material of these two figures carved by Navajos. The larger bear is a fetish, with inlaid eyes and arrow.

contain as many as 100 elephants, camels, and lions in slivers of ivory—the seed being about ⅜ in. (9 mm) in its longest dimension and fitted with an ivory plug to close the open end. I also have from India a regular needle standing in the cork of a vial—with a camel of ivory literally going through the eye. But these are not for tyros or to be made as initial projects.

I have gathered here a variety of examples from a variety of sources. They are not overly difficult; they just require care in wood selection, a sharp eye, a sharp small-bladed knife, and a steady hand.

8

How to Approach a Commission

If you are fortunate enough to get a commission, be very careful to find out what the prospective client has in mind. He or she can request something that is beyond you, or can expect a treatment, subject, or wood that you didn't understand about. If these elements are clear to both parties, you can exercise a great deal of freedom in design and execution.

If some time is spent initially in working out a design that is a challenge to the carver, it stretches his or her skill a little so something can be learned. My clients have been uniformly pleased at the pieces they ultimately received, although the pieces usually varied somewhat from what they expected.

I remember on one occasion I was commissioned to make a four-way head for a doctor in a nearby town. (The four-way head is something I thought I had originated until I saw that the Celts and Mayans 1000 years ago had anticipated me.) Now, a four-way head is relatively simple; it is basically a rectangular block with an eye on each long side and a nose at each corner between. The top can be a sort of doge's headdress or have other variations—I once made one for a Mexican friend who was a quarter Spanish, a quarter Scottish, and half Indian, so the four noses and sections of headdress had to reflect these differences. In this case, the lady was an ardent feminist, so wanted women to be rep-

Figs. 8.1 and 8.2. Queen of hearts, flanked by knave of diamonds on left and king of spades on right, make the four-way head in Fig. 8.1. In Fig 8.2 is the joker, flanked by king of spades on left and knave of diamonds on right. The piece, in teak, is 6 × 6 × 15 in. (152 × 152 × 381 mm) and is on a Lazy Susan, so can be rotated. Note winking eye shared by joker and knave and changes of motif in collars and other designs mid-face. This caused some stewing, but worked out.

Fig. 8.3. Another variation of the four-way head, this time by a student, Hugh Minton, Jr. It is in walnut and adapted for a lamp base. It is drilled through and mounted on ball bearings, so the heads can be rotated independently of the fixture, which acts as an axle.

resented in the work. The only sensible combination I could think of were the faces from a deck of cards: the king of spades, queen of hearts, jack of diamonds, and a joker. I had a suitable 12 × 12 × 24 in. (300 × 300 × 600 mm) block of teak. The clients agreed, so I started in happily to carve the piece.

All sorts of problems turned up. A lady with three men? The queen of hearts is a fearsome creature, according to *Alice in Wonderland*, so she could be somewhat masculine, but I suddenly realized that she must be identified with hearts while the king of spades on one side should have spade motifs and the jack of diamonds on the other side required diamonds. (I was placing the joker at her back because I wanted to have one winking eye to be shared by joker and jack.) Further, the motifs had to be interchanged at the center of a flat face of the block, not at a convenient corner. It took some juggling, but it

could be done and looked fine when finished. Further, the queen's bosom suggested shoulders for adjacent males, and the beards of king and knave suggested decoration on her bodice. Also, the top could be made three-quarters crown, with suitable variations in detail. In finishing, I decided to mount the block on a Lazy Susan or turntable base, so all the faces could be seen conveniently. (One of my students has recently done a lamp with the four-way heads and worked out a somewhat more elaborate ball-bearing mounting, so the four-way head rotates on a central shaft supporting the lamp top.)

As I review the subjects I've carved, I begin to realize that subjects like the preceding one cross the dim line between woodcarving and sculpture, because any worthwhile major piece should include a generous dosage of art.

Another commission was for a panel to be placed in a dental office in Sarasota, Florida, so the dentist wanted something suggesting the circus to go with other elements of his office decor. I had never seen his office nor met him; the commission had come through an intermediary. I guessed immediately that his circus-motif items were probably the familiar prints and paintings showing clowns, animals, and aerialists, so I should undertake something different. So I went to the children's room of our local library to do some research. They had a half-dozen circus books, plus two folders of clipped printed pictures—most of the latter again the familiar ones. But I fell in love with a stylized circus wagon drawn some years back by John Alcorn, and decided to interpret it in low relief. Other sketches of his showed a somewhat stylized matching horse which could be adapted to pull the wagon, and some of the loose pictures suggested the harness arrangement. Also, there was a photograph of an "ironjaw"—the lady aerialist who hangs by her teeth—that intrigued me because perhaps 40 years ago I whittled a three-dimensional ironjaw who serves as the end of a pull-cord on a light switch. I had a new piece of holly about 10 in.

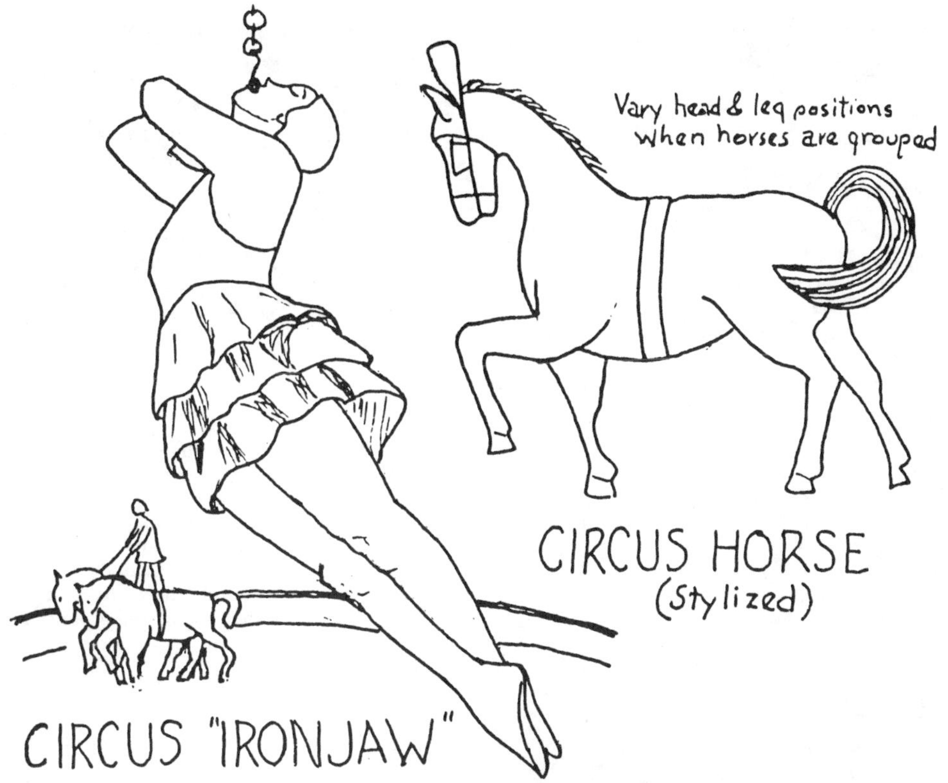

Vary head & leg positions when horses are grouped

CIRCUS HORSE
(Stylized)

CIRCUS "IRONJAW"

(250 mm) wide that would be suitable for her.

The ironjaw was a relatively easy carving, because holly takes detail so well and also provides a very nice finish. So I trench-carved her (meaning that the full ¾ in. (18.75 mm) depth of the board was retained around the edges and the design was set in a central "trench"—an old Egyptian trick). I indulged myself also by leaving the bark on the sides as a sort of half frame and thus avoiding the squared look of most paintings and panels. Finish was a coat or two of sprayed-on satin-finish varnish and "antiquing" with dark-tan Kiwi® shoe polish. She is quite dramatic and satisfies my design.

I remember from my childhood that all circus wagons seemed to be drawn by multiple teams, although some of the pictures belied that, showing fairly ordinary lightly decorated wagons drawn by single teams or even single horses. I decided to have my wagon drawn by two teams. Then I remembered a piece of cherry I had that is 8 in. (200 mm) wide and with so much "figure" it could be called bird's-eye. It was too

Fig. 8.4. Pattern for the "ironjaw."

Fig. 8.5. The "ironjaw," an aerialist who hung by her teeth, was a staple of the three-ring circus. This one is trenched into a section of holly with the bark left on the edges. Overall size is about 10 × 12 in. (254 × 305 mm). To bring out the design, the background and lines are antiqued.

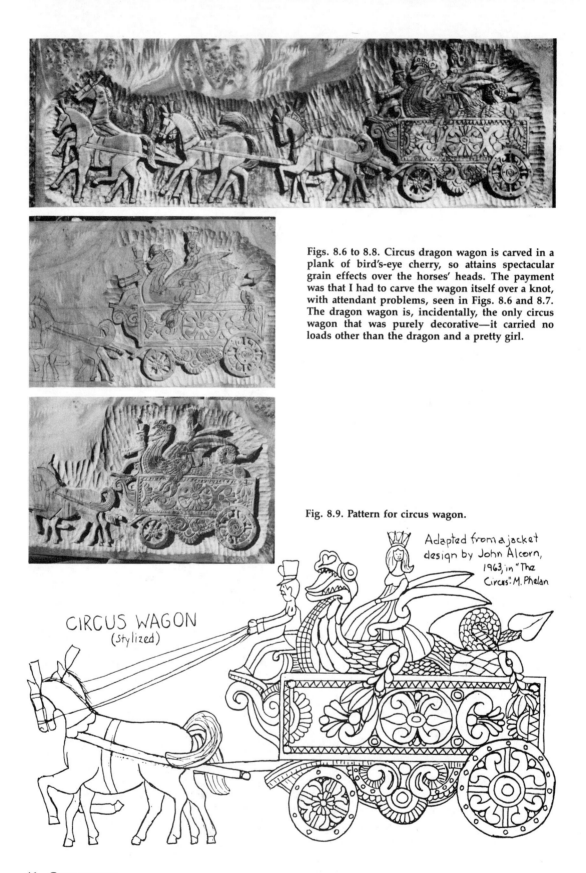

Figs. 8.6 to 8.8. Circus dragon wagon is carved in a plank of bird's-eye cherry, so attains spectacular grain effects over the horses' heads. The payment was that I had to carve the wagon itself over a knot, with attendant problems, seen in Figs. 8.6 and 8.7. The dragon wagon is, incidentally, the only circus wagon that was purely decorative—it carried no loads other than the dragon and a pretty girl.

Fig. 8.9. Pattern for circus wagon.

Adapted from a jacket design by John Alcorn, 1963, in "The Circus": M. Phelan

CIRCUS WAGON
(Stylized)

long for the projected carving, so I added another team—making six horses, and as I realized later, making it necessary to carve 24 legs! However, the elaborately decorated wagon, which had a dragon and lady on top as well as the driver, could be placed over an area with a knot, so that the horse teams could be strung out below the area of much of the swirled grain, which could thus be preserved if I resorted again to trench carving. No sooner said than done, as you can see from Figs. 8.6–8.8. Setting-in was less than ⅛ in. (3 mm) deep, and antiquing again provided accent. I offered the client his choice of the two. He enthusiastically took both.

A carving like the wagon provides many opportunities for originality in the texturing of wagon decoration and the placement of horse heads and feet. The reins are suggested by lines incised in the trenched area—the trenched area being enlarged to permit this. Best of all, the carving can be done with quite simple tools, ⅛- and ½-in. sweep gouges, a small veiner and a ⅛ in. V-tool, plus a pocket knife for detail and a ⅛ in. thin firmer for setting-in. All the tools, in fact, were of the small, inexpensive type.

By now you should understand why commissions intrigue me. They force me to design and to solve problems that I wouldn't have thought of myself. A third, recent example may help explain why I feel as I do.

Thirty-five years ago, we knew a high-school girl here through our son. She moved away, but we have stayed in touch with her through the years. Recently, she and her husband stopped by to visit from California. She decided during her visit that she wanted a carving of mine, and mentioned that the subject would be a 'cellist. She said she'd send a photo, and I agreed, assuming that like so many potential commissions it would die aborning. However, she did send photos—five of them—and I realized for the first time that *she* is the 'cellist!

Because I thought the commission would not be implemented, I didn't think much about the problems involved. But, looking at the photos and remembering what I knew about 'cellos, I realized that I faced a number of problems. How could the bow be depicted so it wouldn't be broken at the first dusting? Should the strings be actual strings of wire, thus subject to rusting, or silver and fragile? What about the support pin at the base? A 'cello is a precise shape, and unless carved very precisely, it will be quite wrong.

Thoughts like these led me to suggest a relief panel rather than an in-the-round piece, because I figured there must be a solution to the problems of supporting the bow and strings, to say nothing of the stool or projecting hand. She'd suggested that I lengthen her dress to the floor—which solved the problem of the support pin nicely in relief. I also suggested several sizes and she picked the largest, 11 × 16 in. (279 × 406 mm). The board I had that large was a 1¼-in. (31-mm) plank end of Honduras mahogany I had rescued from the scrap heap of a nearby house-building project. I'm not fond of mahogany, even Honduras mahogany, because of its tendency to split and splinter, but it does offer a challenge of its own and makes a beautiful finished job. I selected as a base photo for my pattern a sort of three-quarter view, which was more interesting and less static than a full front or full side view, even though I knew it would add the problem of a face partially turned, increase the perspective problems on 'cello and figure, and make difficult the depiction of strings and bridge. However, the bow problem was solved because it could be anchored against the body of the 'cello to give it strength. Further, I realized that I could have at least some part of the 'cello neck and fingerboard against her body, and other elements against her skirt. Also, the mahogany could be finished in relatively light tones, good in this case since the client is a blonde. Walnut would be too dark, butternut too soft, cherry would offer many of the problems of mahogany, and I didn't have a piece of cherry wide enough anyway.

The solution is pictured, complete with pattern, which incidentally was started by enlarging the photo in three steps on a copier, by which time it was so blurred that converting to a drawing was necessary. Then two more enlargements and I had the size I wanted—much easier than the method of squares or point-to-point. (Some things about this world are getting easier!) There was a great deal of experimenting to get the strings to look right. I had planned to incise lines, but I found it better to incise five lines rather than four, and to cut away the wood on the sides, thus suggesting the strings in their roundness rather than representing them by grooves as I've done before. It was impractical to carve under the bow and extended arm, as well as under the fingerboard, so all of these were undercut and darkened in finishing with walnut stain. The background was left rough, showing gouge marks, and also darkened with the stain. Before the darkening, the entire panel was sprayed with matte varnish (so-called satin finish) to seal it (including the back, because mahogany likes to warp). Then the stain was brushed on and immediately wiped, to leave the darker color in the cut lines. Because of the preliminary varnish coat, it was possible to control the color fairly precisely.

At that point, I thought it was done. But I saw that the bridge appeared to slope and a couple of other spots needed redoing. My wife was not pleased with the face, so that required some reworking, mostly rounding and thinning. A neighbor who is a skilled musician added other changes, including a slight increase in the curvature at the center of the 'cello and a correction on the bow. Fortunately, things like this can be corrected—reshape, revarnish, restain, and be certain each step is blended in to match surrounding wood. I also scratched away several spots where the stain had "taken" too darkly, and restained the large area at upper left to make it darker, thus less obtrusive. Final finish was several coats of neutral Kiwi® shoe polish.

I have tried to show the steps in arriving

Fig. 8.10. Mahogany is the wood of this 1¼ × 11 × 16½ in. (31 × 279 × 406 mm) panel of a 'cellist.

Fig. 8.11. Pattern for 'cellist.

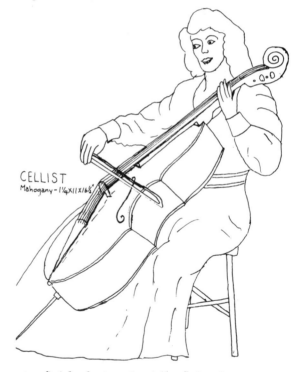

CELLIST
Mahogany - 1¼ X 11 X 16⅛"

at a finished piece in each of the three examples. Each was a challenging problem and taught me some things I didn't know. And there was a real sense of accomplishment when they were accepted (and paid for) with acclaim. I guess that's why I'll always prefer commissions to my own non-commissioned ideas, or worse still, repetitive copying of a tiresome shape or figure because it's a sure sale.

9

Carve Architectural Details

Once you've progressed into relief carving with chisels, you may have calls from architects, cabinetmakers, or interior designers for elements in a decorative scheme. The pattern or specification you receive may be vague at best but the need is usually immediate. One designer needed four pillar capitals to go between semi-columns and formed plaster arches over large bookcases in a refurbished sunroom. The patterns reproduced here represented the interior designer's concept of what they should be. Note the vagueness in details and modelling, the projecting ends of elements and the barely defined swirls. This brings up the first point of importance: *Have it understood between yourself and the client that you should have a bit of latitude in interpreting his sketches.* This is vital because you may discover as you carve that some details do not work out exactly according to the drawing, or you may have slight errors of your own to correct by minor design changes.

The second point of importance is to *know something of the budget.* In this case, the need was for four capitals, but the budget was tight and the designer had access to a man who could make good plaster castings in rubber molds, once he had a suitable pattern. The three plaster copies could be made for just about the cost of one additional woodcarving. (I hesitate to admit it, but I was happy that this was true; the first one was fun . . . but three more?)

The third point of importance is to *know how the carving is to be finished.* In this case,

the piece was to be painted anyway, so I could choose my own wood and finish as I liked, as long as I avoided rough spots and projections that would cause molding problems—or dusting and cleaning problems after installation. So I chose mahogany, which can support this much detail, and avoided several of the fragile sketched projections. The finished carving was given three coats of matte varnish. I antiqued it with dark walnut stain, quickly wiped off area by area in order to darken hollows to accentuate the carving, as pictured. Result: Enthusiastic acceptance by both designer and client.

I was called in on another commission by a cabinetmaker who was designing a pair of doors for a client. The cabinetmaker had suggested two panelled doors for a beach house. His client debated, so he asked me to make a sample in mahogany. To get the folds clear, it was necessary to ground down almost 1 in. (25 mm), using half the depth to get the lower parts of the fold. There was some debate about the framing as well, so my sample was trenched—the cabinetmaker could remove the bordering wood by machine anyway. As it turned out, the customer decided on different doors, so this panel became merely a sample. But it points up another thing to remember: *If you make a sample, charge for it,* or you may lose out. And further: Don't count your chickens before they're hatched! Some jobs never come through.

Fig. 9.1. This capital is in mahogany, 2½ × 4 × 5½ in. (64 × 102 × 139 mm). John Collin's sketches allowed considerable carving freedom, essential in handling a rounded shape like this. It was carved from a longer blank which provided clamp space.

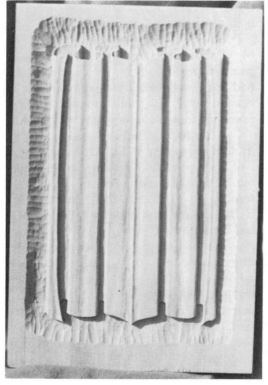

Fig. 9.2. Sample made for a door panel.

Figs. 9.3 to 9.5 (opposite page). Sketches supplied by the interior designer were by no means blueprints or precise patterns—they were intended to provide a feeling or act as a general guide to the woodcarver. Compare the sketches and photograph to see some of the variations I felt were necessary—and were accepted without question. Fig. 9.5 shows the shape of the spandrel where it meets the capital, and the half or false pillar below. These help in determining edge detail, so there are no impossible joinings.

Part 2
In Our Own Backyard:
Designs from the U.S.A.

10

Some Reliefs at Brasstown

Relief carving is extremely versatile in that everything from a single and simple subject to a very complex scene can be depicted by a variety of techniques ranging from the equivalent of a pencilled outline to a scene with elements in the round. In its simpler forms, a single tool like a V-tool or a veiner can be used to cut a design on any reasonably smooth surface, whether or not it is a plane, a cylinder, or whatever. There are endless variations of simple relief carving like diaper work (a diamond-shaped network with varying units inside), chip carving (a repeated pattern of triangular notches usually done with a chisel-like knife), and incising (designs created by shallow grooving).

The next step up in difficulty is a modelled figure or shape, which may be silhouetted or within the borders of a panel. Carving may range from very shallow to quite deep—almost in the round. There are also many ways of treating a panel. The carving may be carved below the panel surface (trenched). The carving may project within a frame. The sides may be cut away to leave the carving standing out. Or the entire carving may be made "inside out" in intaglio—really a mold. In all of these a greater number of tools is used and more skill is required. High relief or deep carving is least stressful because the third dimension is largely present, and the only problem in design is perspective, if it is necessary. As you progress through medium relief to shallow relief or low relief, however, perspective becomes more im-

Fig. 10.1. Dave Peters from North Carolina picked up my challenge to make something of a piece of scrap locust. It shows Egyptian influence, I think, although the dagger is Roman or European, the costume is monkish, and the head is a whatever. But Dave, who is a psychologist, has also carved geese with two heads or a knot in the neck and a variety of other offbeat pieces, as well as encouraging me by buying some of my misdeeds.

portant and much attention must be paid to texture, modelling, and perspective to be certain that elements do not look flat, almost smashed down.

For some reason unbeknownst to me, a fairly large percentage of my students elect to do low-relief carving at the summer course I teach at Brasstown, although there are no limitations placed on their selections. Pictured here are some of their choices (all, by coincidence, reliefs) from the John C. Campbell Folk School in Brasstown, North Carolina. I have for some years tried to teach the class as one in

which the students are all relatively skilled (some can beat me) and can select their own projects. It's hard on my feet and back, but much more fascinating to me, and provides a diversity of design ideas which you may find helpful and intriguing. It is only fair to point out that these pictures do not show the work of the entire class, but only those examples of which I was able to get suitable black-and-white photographs. Some date back, but most are from the 1986 class. Elsewhere, there are pictures of the works of other students, including the usual number who surpass the teacher.

Most of the students are quite mature, some approaching retirement or actually retired, although that is by no means a prerequisite. Also, most of them have had some years of whittling, and in some cases years of relief carving as well. Some have had extensive art training; some have had none. Some are naturals and some are not. (The work of the latter is not included here—after all, I'm bragging.) Most pieces are relatively low relief, but there are some examples of high or medium relief. Most are self-evident and the design can be copied from the photograph as readily as from a drawing.

Figs. 10.2 to 10.4. Many students turn out three panels in the two weeks, but C. L. Sturgeon, who is a carving teacher in Louisiana, did these three exceptionally good ones. They include an Indian, an eagle, and a deer family.

Fig. 10.5. J. Rooney Floyd, a Georgia engineer, has carved several pieces including a child's hand grasping a parent's finger, but this is all I have to show. It is a portrait of the gaillardia in walnut in medium relief, taken from the designs of H. M. Sutter.

Fig. 10.6. Mike Horrick, a fellow Hoosier, did this Madonna and Child in holly as his second relief. We almost ruined it in the finishing, but it is still a lovely piece.

Fig. 10.7. An Italian named Ghiberti spent most of his lifetime carving a dozen panels to be cast in bronze for a church in Florence. About 18 × 24 in. (450 × 600 mm), this is a mahogany copy of one of the panels by Robert Pansius of South Carolina, showing the baptism of Jesus. It is in medium relief.

Fig. 10.8. James Whiting of Florida and North Carolina challenges me each year to come up with a design he'll have trouble doing. This is his 1986 piece—wild ginger in cherry wood. The flower stems are completely undercut, as are the leaf edges.

Fig. 10.9. I showed the work of Dr. W. L. Collette in *Woodcarver's Pattern & Design Book* (1986), but Bill has a habit of coming up with something even better. This one he called "Curtain Call." It is in tulip poplar 1¾ × 31 × 32 in. (43.75 × 775 × 800 mm). Note how he has "broken" the frame to project his figure, the excellent handling of foreshortening and perspective, and above all the hands and face.

Figs. 10.10 and 10.11 (top). Darrell Rhudy produced these two (among four) panels, one a fairly deep relief of stylized flowers in yellow pine (a difficult wood), the other an exceptional flying owl in an old barn board. The owl has carved feathers and a chip-carved breast. The board itself was gray, of course, but carving the circle gave a yellow moon background.

Figs. 10.12 to 10.14. Jill Ruane wanted to carve a shell copied from one impressed on a bar of soap. Here is her version, in holly, as well as two in-the-round tortoises in basswood, one partially finished, the other almost alive, as visitors remarked. Back markings are done with a pyrographic needle. Jill raises turtles. She also did a stylized peacock in a slab of silky oak.

Fig. 10.15. Doris Irwin combined carving and pyrography to produce this interesting scene of raccoons in cherry.

Fig. 10.16. Judi Hickson produced this low-relief adaptation of a Cherokee painting in cherry. It is a snowy owl flying in the moonlight, with a mystic Indian head modelled on its wing.

Figs. 10.17 and 10.18. Jeff Swain, a modelmaker learning carving, carved four panels, of which these two in walnut were quite good. One is a study of roses, the other a copy of a design by C. L. Sturgeon.

11

The Mountains Breed Carvers

Western North Carolina has always had mountain and Cherokee carvers—a rare concurrence of two cultures, particularly because they do not usually overlap. The mountain people carve animals and human figures with which they are familiar; the Cherokees carve masks and Indian figures in wood, and mystic and realistic miniature statuary in soft stone.

My hobby of collecting Cherokee stone carved miniatures led to the discovery that there is a largely exhausted soapstone (steatite) mine only seven miles from the Campbell Folk School in Brasstown, North Carolina, where I teach every year. As a result, students made several excursions to the mine and brought back about 500 pounds of soft stone. Much of it disappeared into the students' conveyances, but some was whittled in class. We had turtles, fish, thunderbugs, and other small pieces, of which the most popular was the thunderbug, from an original I had just purchased in Cherokee. Franklin Owle, who carved it, explained that the Thunderbug bites people who tell lies and will not let go until there is thunder. Franklin was also the source for the information about the mine—although his bug was in red pipestone. The Thunderbug and the coelacanth (a "living fossil" fish) are patterned here if you want to try them.

The existence of the Folk School has intensified local carving. Many local people carve as a hobby and market through the Folk School. Of these the carvings most in demand are by Ruth Hawkins, almost al-

Fig. 11.1. The Thunderbug, here in red pipestone by Franklin Owle, bites liars and will not let go until it thunders, according to legend. It is 2½ in. (64 mm) long, and was popular in my class for copying in either stone or wood.

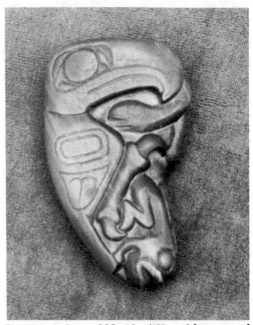

Fig. 11.2. A river pebble 4 in. (102 mm) long, carved with interlacing figures, is typical of the Wilnotys, Cherokee carvers. This one is by J. J. Wilnoty II.

Fig. 11.3. These four figures in holly are by Ruth Hawkins, who is peerless in carving angelic child faces. They include Mary and Joseph, a flute-playing "angel," and one of the Nativity shepherds with a lamb. Joseph is 4½ in. (115 mm) tall.

Fig. 11.4. Hen in butternut and rabbit in buckeye are by Sue McClure. The hen is 3½ in. (89 mm) long.

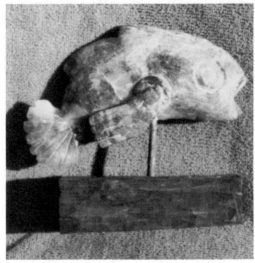

Fig. 11.5. "Coelacanth," by Judi Hickson, is in steatite (soapstone) which is green in color. The stone comes from a local mine near Brasstown, N.C.

MARY & JOSEPH

FLUTIST

DRUMMER

SHEPHERD BOY
All in Holly ¼" thick

FIVE FIGURES   Ruth Hawkins, Warne, N.C.

Judi Hickson N.Y.

Soapstone COELECANTH

Franklin Owle, Cherokee, N.C.
THUNDERBUG-pipestone red

HEN in Butternut
TWO ANIMALS
Sue McClure, Warne, N.C.

RABBIT in Buckeye

Fig. 11.6. Patterns for Sue McClure and Ruth Hawkins figures, coelacanth and thunderbug.

ways in holly and about ¼ in. (6 mm) thick. Four of her newer ones are pictured and patterned. Another mountain carver is Sue McClure, who is famous for her chickens, ducks, bears, hounds, and deer. A rabbit in buckeye and a hen in butternut are illustrated here.

I have also sketched and photographed a few of the pieces carved by Wade Martin, who lived somewhere near Asheville, North Carolina, and may still be alive, although not carving—nobody seems to know exactly. In any case, these are portraits (not caricatures) of his family and friends, of hounds and a rabbit, that are honest, straightforward—and different. He finished these pieces without color, and he had no consistent scale or treatment—he whittled what he saw.

Fig. 11.7. Boy with gun and pup at left is said to be a self-portrait of Wade Martin, and the country fiddler beside him a portrait of his father. Each is about 8 in. (203 mm) tall.

Fig. 11.8. The woman with children was probably Wade's mother, and the seated whittler a self-portrait. The latter is one piece, including the stool.

Fig. 11.9. Blacksmith and anvil are to a different scale than the other figures—probably because that was the piece of wood that came to hand. (Here the anvil was closer to the camera, so is out of scale with the smith.) Next to the blacksmith is a moonshiner about 8 in. (203 mm) tall, a familiar figure of past years—and on occasion, of the present. Note that this is again a portrait, not a caricature.

Fig. 11.9. Hounds look familiar, but these are live poses, not static ones. Consider the very dejected 2 in. (51 mm) pup who is carved cross-grain in a strongly grained wood (my guess is fir).

Fig. 11.10. In contrast to the thin and rough-finished hounds, this jackrabbit is fat and sleek. He is about 4 in. (102 mm) long, and in pecan.

Fig. 11.11. Patterns for Wade Martin figures.

12

Mountain Carver—Plus

Hal McClure, now in his mid-30's, is a North Carolina mountain carver—and the fourth generation of a family that has made its living that way. He is basically self-taught and learned carving by "osmosis," he says, from his mother Sue, who is a famous carver in Appalachia. He sold his first carving at age four, but has really been a pro for only a bit over ten years. (He got a quarter for that first carving—and demanded payment by check, because that's how his mother was paid.) Hal carves bears, foxes, hounds, panthers, turtles, mountain people—typical mountain pieces, but his have an extra flair—they *live*. He sells 90% of his work wholesale, through such outlets as the John C. Campbell Folk School, the Southern Highlands Handicraft Guild, and a number of private galleries and shops. He has had shows and demonstrations all over the East. He has taught at the Folk School for several years,

Fig. 12.1. Hal McClure with children in a school class.

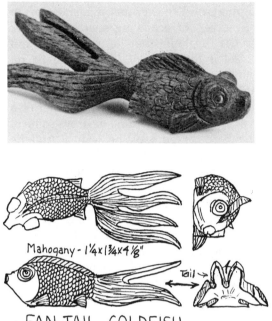

FAN-TAIL GOLDFISH

Mahogany - 1¼ x ¾ x 4⅛"

Figs. 12.2 and 12.3. Oriental goldfish in mahogany is ¾ × 2 in. (16.5 mm × 51 mm) and takes an hour to carve with pocketknife and palm gouges.

Fig. 12.4. Medicine man in local steatite (soapstone), complete with eagle headdress, is 2 in. (51 mm) tall and 1½ in. (28 mm) long. Carving time is 6 hours. Tools are coping saw, rasp, and homemade gouges.

and more recently at schools in and around Franklin, North Carolina, where he lives. For the past three years he has been artist-in-the-school for the Macon County Board of Education in schools in the Franklin area. This program is funded partly by the North Carolina Arts Council and partly by the National Endowment for the Arts. It was created to instill in mountain children some feeling for traditions and native crafts. It is not lecturing, but "hands on" teaching. He has no capacious home studio—his shop is about 10 × 14 feet (3.05 × 3.56 m) in a very small house—and it includes bandsaw, drill press and grinder. But everything in it is within easy reach, except for wood. Much of that he buys in quantity as needed, and some he raids from his mother's woodpile back in Warne, North Carolina.

He has a considerable itch to try something new, which is how we met ten years ago when he began relief carving. He tries to make each carving better than its predecessor, and when he can no longer improve it, he tends to abandon it for a newer

Fig. 12.5. "The Frontiersman" is in cherry, ⅞ × 7¾ × 21½ in. (22 × 197 × 540 mm). The design was adapted to fit the wood, which had the curving top that suggested a tree. Detailing is used only where essential. Carving depth is only ⅛ in. (3 mm). You can't buy it—it's mine.

design. This works to his advantage, of course, because he regularly has something new to offer to clients. He also works in many woods, including mahogany, buckeye, holly, walnut, butternut, cherry, and even stone—the latter being steatite, or red pipestone like the Cherokees carve. He also likes to reduce the size of a piece— he has made bears that will pass through a wedding ring and are still very detailed. He has no desire to go the other way, however, to heroic figures, nor to undertake formal or architectural carving. His animals and people are always in natural poses and are realistic: He wants the work to look as if the subject were caught in mid-movement.

Hal is the most competent man with a coping saw I've ever met, which is part of his secret for achieving speed. His basic tool is the knife, but he uses mallet and chisel if there's a lot of wood to be removed. A V-tool and stamps put eyes in animal figures. He doesn't sand unless the subject must be sleek, like a panther or a fish; he feels that sanding destroys some of the hard-carved look he wants. And he tells his youngest students his philosophy: "Carve what your mind sees, nothing more or less. You know what your mind sees, and only you can make something of it."

Hal has been generous, letting me publish a number of his blank shapes—the first step in saving time. The photos of his work here are by John Dailey, Fred Eldredge, Joann Jones, and yours truly.

Fig. 12.6. Black-walnut trivet is ¾ in. (19 mm) thick and 7½ in. (190 mm) from side to side. Relief carving is about ¼ in. (6 mm) deep. It is done with palm gouges in about 6 hours.

Fig. 12.7. Bear is in ivory—one of Hal's experiments. It is about 1½ in. (39 mm) long, and was probably appropriated by his wife, Jan.

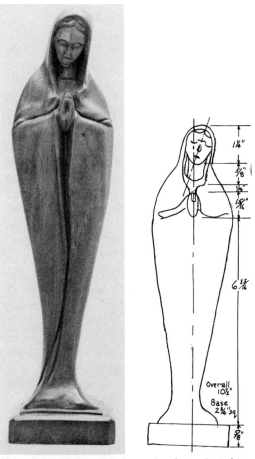

Figs. 12.8 and 12.9. Madonna in cherry is 1 foot (305 mm) tall and takes 8 hours to carve and sand. The bandsawed blank is finished with coping saw and pocketknife.

Fig. 12.10 and 12.11. Mountain man and woman are in cherry, 9 in. (228 mm) tall. They take 8 hours each from bandsawed blanks, using palm chisels and pocketknife.

Fig. 12.12. Sitting and running black-walnut bears are only 1¾ in. (43 mm) tall and 2⅜ in. (61 mm) long. They are produced with bandsaw, pocketknife, and palm gouges in 45 minutes each.

Fig. 12.13. Box turtle in butternut is 1 in. (25 mm) tall by 2¾ in. (68 mm) long, takes 1½ hours with coping saw and pocketknife.

Fig. 12.14. Panther or "painter" is in cherry and a limited-edition piece—only five are to be made. Time to carve and sand is 8 hours. It is 4 × 12 in. (102 × 308 mm).

Fig. 12.15. Red fox is in cherry, 4½ × 8 in. (117 × 203 mm). It takes 2½ hours. Tools are bandsaw, coping saw, and pocketknife.

Fig. 12.16. Tree spirit is in cherry, 24 in. (610 mm) tall. It is done entirely with chisels, and of course no two faces are alike. It takes 1¼ hours.

Fig. 12.17. Horned owl in buckeye is 8¾ in. (216 mm) tall and takes 4 hours. It is done with coping saw, pocketknife and palm gouges.

13

Engineer Carves for Children

John C. Boyles of Jacksonville, Florida, is a retired railroad civil-engineer and a long-time carver. In a sense, he has known me longer than I've known him—he bought one of my books about 30 years ago, but he first came to my class at the Campbell Folk School in 1985, shortly after one of several heart attacks. He has had bypass surgery since, but is still an indomitable carver, heavily involved in making toy boxes, cradles, and the like for his grandchildren. He does his research for designs, and adapts from photographs or drawings, but in a pinch makes his own designs to suit the need. These are a few examples of his meticulous and whimsical work.

Fig. 13.1. A Madonna in walnut, done as a low-relief project in class.

Fig. 13.2. Deep undercutting characterizes this orchid panel in teak, adapted from a design by H. M. Sutter of Portland, Oregon. This is very intricate.

Fig. 13.3. Dahlias are the subject of this low-relief walnut panel. The design is taken from H. M. Sutter's book, *Floral Wood Carving*, Dover, N.Y., 1985.

Figs. 13.4 to 13.10. Seven carved elements from various toy boxes and a cradle made by Jack. Several of the cradle designs were taken from photos in a "Chip Chats" article by Paul Wright on how to make a cradle, and the locomotive came from original research—like all railroad men, Jack is fascinated by old engines.

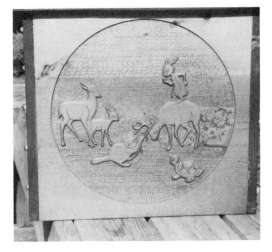

Figs. 13.11 and 13.12. Three figures in ¼ in. (6 mm) holly include an angel taken from a Ruth Hawkins original, a child with a candle, and a stiff "wooden"

TWO FIGURES in ¼" Holly

soldier. Pieces like this he whittles in the hospital while recovering from heart problems.

Fig. 13.13. For a granddaughter's doll house, these miniature chairs are meticulous whittling projects to scale. One has a solid seat, the other a caned one.

Fig. 13.14. Gnome with pipe, requiring some careful cutting.

Fig. 13.15. Patterns.

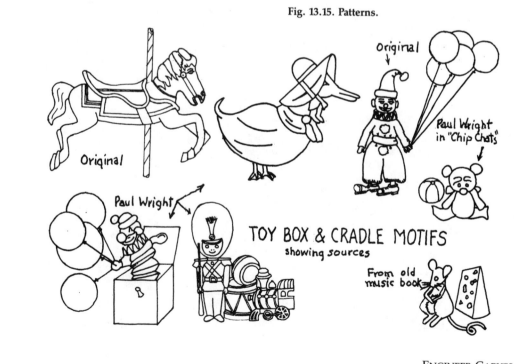

14

From Sketches to Sculpture

Some of us have been carving since childhood, but more have undertaken the craft only as they approached retirement. This latter fact has frequently been offered as an excuse for mediocre works. It has little merit, as these examples show. They're the work of Ralph H. Bower of Goshen, Indiana, who began carving in 1975 when he was 60 years old and a partner in a thriving business unrelated to woodcarving. He was interested in carving long before that, however, stimulated by such things as figures of an Amish couple carved by a fellow Hoosier named Jerome Frye. (I showed pictures of them in my first books 50 years ago.) He'd even bid on a set of tools in 1956. Had his bid been accepted, he might well have started carving that much sooner.

There are several unusual elements in his approach. He has no art background and is entirely self-taught. However, his father had a printing business and he spent 25 years in specialty printing, so he was exposed to layout and design from the start. As a carver, he set himself challenging projects from the beginning, that of converting drawings, paintings, and pho-

Fig. 14.1. The perpetrator and some of his pieces—the leprechaun unpainted but very visible, a symbol of the man behind it.

tographs of work by artists he admires into three dimensions. He does *not* copy statues, or other carving as such. He does do some original pieces, but conversion intrigues him more. He confesses to a particular interest in the medieval, and feels that Riemenschneider and Stöss may be looking over his shoulder as he works— and agrees that he still has much to learn to achieve the best of which he is capable. He has had occasional showings, including a one-man show of 65 of his pieces some years back, but he sells very little and accepts only commissions that intrigue him beyond his resistance. Although I've known him for some years, he has denied me permission to show his work until now.

The photographs here show the extraordinarily wide range of his work and his versatility, as well as his penchant for the fragile. Much of what he does is finished by painting, but it ranges from an untinted head of Christ to intricate patterns (taken from Disney blueprints) for the old-fashioned lamp post capitals in Disney World in Florida. And he continues to seek variety and challenge.

Fig. 14.2. "In memory of Kate B. Hay, Fowler librarian, 1921–1948" reads the brass plate on this carving of an old nursery rhyme as drawn by Arthur Rackham. Ms. Hay is fondly remembered by Ralph Bower as a woman who did much to influence youth—including himself as a youngster in his hometown. The plaque hangs in the Benton County Public Library, Fowler, Indiana.

Figs. 14.3 and 14.4. "Puck" is taken from the drawings of Brian Froud in a book titled "Faeries" (Harry N. Abrams, Inc., N.Y., 1978). This is a very difficult conversion of an intricate design.

Figs. 14.5 and 14.6. A further sketch by Froud inspired "Leap Frog"—this complex piece. Ralph's copies are colored and a foot or more tall. They require a delicate and steady hand, among other attributes. (These drawings are reproduced with Mr. Froud's permission.)

Fig. 14.7. Comparing the African-inspired piece with this Indian chief illustrates the diversity of Mr. Bower's work. The Indian is based on an 1833 watercolor by Karl Bodmer, but the face came from a photograph of Chief Joseph.

Fig. 14.8. This African style piece is the result of a need for a small table in a new house of the Bowers. He seldom carves from logs because he feels they are too unstable for his usual delicate work, but this log had been presented by a fellow carver and seemed right for the piece. The design was copied from a book on African art which Mrs. Bower happened to buy.

Figs. 14.9 and 14.10. Ralph's current project at this writing is taken from an etching by Albrecht Dürer, dated 1523. It will be in high relief on a 3¾ × 27 × 35 in. (95 × 686 × 889 mm) panel of Honduras mahogany.

Fig. 14.11. Close-up of the head of Christ made for a doctor in Goshen is from a painting by Warner Sollman in 1940, but Ralph found it "somewhat diffuse and impressionistic" in copying. When completed, it was framed with a Gothic-screen headpiece from Riemenschneider adapted to suit.

Fig. 14.12. This portly dancing couple was based on a small element in a painting by the Colombian artist Botero, who is also a sculptor. It shows Ralph's skill at depicting action and verve.

Figs. 14.13 and 14.14. "Leprechaun" is also based on a Brian Froud sketch in "Faeries." The toadstools and base are Bower additions.

Fig. 14.15. The Hessian soldier (below, left) is actually a whirligig with arms that rotate in a breeze, so he has two signal flags to balance the arms rather than the one that's historically correct. The arms can be locked in opposed positions for whirling. In basswood, he is 23½ in. (597 mm) tall plus base, in accurate costume except possibly for helmet details. The Shaker Woman (below, center) is in basswood and 20 in. (508 mm) tall. She is based on Shaker photographs and the loan of a Shaker cloak from the museum at Pleasant Hill, Kentucky. The colonial U.S. Marine (below, right) is basswood, 24 in. (610 mm) tall, plus a 4 in. (102 mm) stand. He is based on a drawing in a children's book and is authentic in detail, but has lost his bayonet.

Fig. 14.16. "Girl with Muff," a basswood carving based on a figure in a Sir Joshua Reynolds painting. The figure is 19½ in. (290 mm) tall on a 2-in. (51 mm) base. The original painting was altered slightly in this figure to give it a folk-art quality. The real challenge was the hat.

Fig. 14.17 (above right). "Lady in a Breeze" in basswood is also based on Ed Gorey's work. The figures are 12½ in. (318 mm) tall (including stand). It is finished with natural shoe polish. (Ralph adds the caution that oil stain works better than colored shoe polish to apply a tint.) He heats the polish with a heat gun, puts on more than necessary, then lets it soak in before he wipes it down and polishes the piece. This avoids the "shiny" look that we both deplore.

Figs. 14.18 and 14.19. Another of Brian Froud's delightful and complex figures transferred to three dimensions and tinted after completion. This is very difficult and challenging—note the slight variations in hair, hat, hands and face.

15

State Birds, Trees, and Flowers

The leaders of our 50 states have, at one time or another, seen fit to adopt particular birds as state symbols, just as they have selected a tree and a flower. Some of these make good sense, such as the nene goose for Hawaii, the loon for Minnesota, the willow ptarmigan for Alaska, the cactus wren for Arizona, and the roadrunner for New Mexico. These are not common birds and they are best known, or even exclusively known, in their home states. But others, like the cardinal, selected by seven states; the mockingbird, selected by five states; or the western meadowlark, selected by six states, seem to suggest that leaders, too, can be unimaginative—or at least not "up" on their birds.

Some time back, a friend and I did a checkup on appropriate woods for birds. They included cedar for the cedar waxwing, black ash for blackbirds, redwood for cardinals, pussy willow for catbirds, blue spruce for bluebirds, sage for sage hens, canary wood for canaries, purpleheart for the purple martin, scarlet haw for the scarlet tanager, beefwood for the cowbird, sapwood for the sapsucker, growth wood for the pee wee, and maybe horse chestnut for sparrows and mesquite for the Texas state "bird," the mosquito. But in this instance, I abandoned all that for a panel of walnut and a Christmas idea.

When I discovered that our 50 states have selected only a total of 28 birds among them, I decided to make a polyglot grouping of them in the form of a Christmas tree, the resulting panel to be used on my Christmas card. The panel was quite a

Fig. 15.1. A walnut panel combines the 28 birds of our 50 states into a Christmas-tree form. I tried to avoid feet (a nuisance!) and to use characteristic poses and silhouettes for ready identification. It could have been made with tree leaves or flowers (see accompanying table).

STATE BIRDS AS A CHRISTMAS TREE Walnut 1x10x15½"
Jan., 1986

Fig. 15.2. Pattern for State Birds panel.

Key for State Birds Panel

1. Carolina Wren—South Carolina
2. Scissor-Tailed Flycatcher—Oklahoma
3. Black-Capped Chickadee—Maine,
   Massachusetts
4. Cardinal—Illinois, Indiana, Kentucky,
   North Carolina, Ohio, Virginia, West Virginia
5. Brown Pelican—Louisiana
6. American Robin—Connecticut,
   Michigan, Wisconsin
7. Ring-Necked Pheasant—South Dakota
8. Rhode Island Red—Rhode Island
9. Blue Hen Chicken—Delaware
10. Eastern Bluebird—Missouri, New York
11. Mountain Bluebird—Idaho, Nevada
12. Mockingbird—Arkansas, Florida,
    Mississippi, Tennessee, Texas
13. Nene Goose—Hawaii
14. Roadrunner—New Mexico

15. Western Meadowlark—Kansas, Montana,
    Nebraska, North Dakota, Oregon, Wyoming
16. American Goldfinch—Iowa, New Jersey,
    Washington
17. Northern (Baltimore) Oriole—Maryland
18. Brown Thrasher—Georgia
19. Cactus Wren—Arizona
20. Willow Ptarmigan—Alaska
21. Ruffed Grouse—Pennsylvania
22. Yellow-Shafted Flicker (Yellow Hammer)—
    Alabama
23. Purple Finch—New Hampshire
24. California Gull—Utah
25. California Quail—California
26. Hermit Thrush—Vermont
27. Lark Bunting—Colorado
28. Common Loon—Minnesota

success; it occasioned a great deal of comment among "birders," particularly after it was one of the first items sold at a one-man show.

The picture and diagram tell the story of design and arrangement. The piece of walnut was $1 \times 10 \times 15\frac{1}{2}$ (25 × 254 × 381 mm) and carving depth is only about $\frac{1}{8}$ in. (3 mm). Bird beaks and tails provide suggestions of fir-branch tips, and there are relatively few obscuring crossovers. Such a panel could, of course, be painted for easier identification of species, but would make a somewhat gaudy array, besides which it seems almost criminal to color walnut. Therefore, I attempted to utilize texture and pose to assist in identification, particularly of birds that have a common shape, such as goldfinches or bluebirds. The wren, with its tendency to stick its tail in the air, was my choice for the top end. The ground birds seemed to gravitate to the bottom. In general, I made an effort to avoid exposing the feet of any bird, because they are a nuisance to carve and would only add to the complications.

My choice was to self-frame the carving, allowing an occasional bird to "break the frame" near the base. The design could have been trench-carved, of course, or finished with flat background for possible exterior framing. It was antiqued with dark walnut stain over matte varnish to emphasize the texturing and other carved lines.

State Trees and Flowers

State	Flower	Tree
Alabama	Camellia	Southern Pine
Alaska	Forget-me-not	Sitka Spruce
Arizona	Saguaro Cactus	Paloverde
Arkansas	Apple Blossom	Pine
California	Golden Poppy	California Redwood
Colorado	Rocky Mountain Columbine	Colorado Blue Spruce
Connecticut	Mountain Laurel	White Oak
Delaware	Peach Blossom	American Holly
Florida	Orange Blossom	Sabal Palmetto Palm
Georgia	Cherokee Rose	Live Oak
Hawaii	Hibiscus	Candlenut
Idaho	Syringa	White Pine
Illinois	Native Violet	White Oak
Indiana	Peony	Tulip Poplar
Iowa	Wild Rose	Oak
Kansas	Native Sunflower	Cottonwood
Kentucky	Goldenrod	Kentucky Coffee Tree
Louisiana	Magnolia	Cypress
Maine	White Pine Cone & Tassel	Eastern White Pine
Maryland	Black-eyed Susan	White Oak
Massachusetts	Mayflower	American Elm
Michigan	Apple Blossom	White Pine
Minnesota	Pink & White Lady's Slipper	Red Pine
Mississippi	Magnolia	Magnolia
Missouri	Hawthorn	Dogwood
Montana	Bitterroot	Ponderosa Pine
Nebraska	Goldenrod	Cottonwood
Nevada	Sagebrush	Single-leaf Piñon
New Hampshire	Purple Lilac	White Birch
New Jersey	Purple Violet	Red Oak
New Mexico	Yucca	Piñon
New York	Rose	Sugar Maple
North Carolina	Dogwood	Pine
North Dakota	Wild Prairie Rose	American Elm
Ohio	Scarlet Carnation	Buckeye
Oklahoma	Mistletoe	Redbud
Oregon	Oregon Grape	Douglas Fir
Pennsylvania	Mountain Laurel	Hemlock
Rhode Island	Violet	Red Maple
South Carolina	Carolina Jessamine	Palmetto
South Dakota	Pasque Flower	Black Hills Spruce
Tennessee	Iris	Tulip Poplar
Texas	Bluebonnet	Pecan
Utah	Sego Lily	Blue Spruce
Vermont	Red Clover	Sugar Maple
Virginia	Dogwood	Dogwood
Washington	Western Rhododendron	Western Hemlock
West Virginia	Big Rhododendron	Sugar Maple
Wyoming	Indian Paintbrush	Cottonwood
Wisconsin	Wood Violet	Sugar Maple
Puerto Rico	Maga	Reinita
Guam	Toto	Ifit (Intsidbijuga)
Virgin Islands	Yellow Elder or Yellow Cedar	None

16

Mother Goose Rhymes

Santa Claus is the dominant spirit at Christmas, but Mother Goose is a year-round presence to children, as well as to the hearts of many adults. So it was only natural that my series of four panels of Arthur Rackham fairy-tale illustrations would lead me into a panel of Mother Goose scenes also taken from his work. In the course of preparing for it, I also found another newer book by Marguerite d'Angeli, with a style I liked—so I ended up with two panels in imbuya, which closely resembles walnut. Both are 1 × 11½ × 22½ in.   (25 × 292 × 571.5 mm).   The Rackham panel has 23 subjects, the d'Angeli one 21, with some adaptation to fit my

available spaces. Most book illustrations are drawn to fit a particular size and shape, and this can be inconvenient in carving dimensions, so on occasion I select just the core of a larger illustration to suit my purposes. Also, it is necessary to work out for each illustration how to make the carving while still retaining the artist's intent. For example, for Little Miss Muffet (12, Rackham) I carved her and the spider in relief, but incised the spider webs and legs of the background. Again, in The Old Woman Who Lived in a Shoe (23, Rackham) I changed the positions and numbers of some children. Also, in This Little Pig (18, Rackham), I used only the pig going to

Fig. 16.1. Nancy Lechner was at work on this depiction of Rackham's "Hot Cross Buns" when this picture was taken. She carved somewhat deeper than I do to accommodate the ribbons, skirts, hands, etc. Note the nice use of trenching and the accuracy of her copy. The wood is cherry.

Fig. 16.2. John Boyles adapted the Rackham illustrations for "Five Little Pigs," placing one pig at the tip of each of his fingers. The wood is walnut, and the hand was life-size. Again, trenching was effective in centering attention.

market—but carver Jack Boyles remedied that by using them all. And Nancy Lechner carved as a single panel one that I regrettably couldn't crowd in. That is one problem; the books have many more illustrations than you can use in any one panel. It should be emphasized that illustrations can be the subjects of individual panels. Or if you prefer some other illustrator, be my guest! (Or your library's.)

Remember the usefulness of relief carving when you want to show a scene rather

Figs. 16.3 to 16.6. Arthur Rackham illustrations were the basis of the left-hand page panel, Marguerite d'Angeli drawings for the one on the right-hand page, in each case from their books of Mother Goose rhymes. The only duplication is in Mother Goose herself at top right and top left, respectively. The wood is imbuya, very much like walnut, and both panels are 11½ × 22½ in. (292 × 571 mm).

Key for Arthur Rackham Mother Goose Panel

1. Old Mother Hubbard
2. Jack Be Nimble
3. Mother Goose
4. Humpty Dumpty
5. Hickory, Dickory Dock
6. The Fly Shall Marry the Bumble-bee
7. Baa, Baa, Black sheep
8. Polly Put the Kettle On
9. Little Jack Horner
10. See Saw, Marjorie Daw
11. Hush-a-Bye Baby
12. Little Miss Muffet
13. The Way We Wash Our Hands
14. Frog He Would a-Wooing
15. Dr. Foster Went to Gos
16. Pussy's in the Well
17. Wee Willie Winkie
18. This Little Pig Went to Market
19. Ride a Cock Horse
20. Tom, Tom, the Piper's Son/Stole a Pig
21. Three Wise Men of G
22. Little Bo-Peep
23. Woman Who Lived in a Shoe

than an individual. Also remember that it can be quite shallow and still be effective; mine were about ⅛ in. (3 mm) deep. And lastly, remember that books and magazines are tremendous sources for ideas and patterns.

Actual carving is not particularly difficult, although it should be as painstaking as you can make it. As faces are usually caricatures anyway, you can approximate the artist's concept and be near enough. If you are carving and don't expect to finish with color, you may have to change texture or shading in your carving.

I find the miniature tools very helpful in doing a carving of this kind. I usually set-in with a ⅛-in. (3-mm) firmer unless I'm doing long straight lines, in which case a ¼-in. (6-mm) or even ½ in. (13 mm) firmer gives a straighter line faster. Also, for very

Key For Marguerite d'Angeli Mother Goose Panel

1. Monday's Child
2. Mother Goose
3. I Love Little Kitty
4. Where Are You Going, My Pretty Maid
5. Three Men in a Tub
6. House Jack Built
7. Hey Diddle Diddle
8. My Son John
9. Little Boy Blue
10. Peter, Peter
11. Goosey Gander
12. Find a Pin
13. Hush-a-Bye, Baby
14. Jack and Jill
15. Three Little Kittens
16. Was a Crooked Man
17. Old King Cole
18. A Fox Jumped Up
19. Old Woman Tossed Up in a Basket
20. 4 & 20 Blackbirds
21. Georgie, Porgie

Fig. 16.7. Step 1—I usually start at one corner of a panel, doing modelling as I go to vary the monotony of grounding. Here my d'Angeli panel is under way. Time: 3 hours plus 3 hours preparation.

Fig. 16.8. Step 2—Here I am progressing downward, with six illustrations modelled and several others set in. The top of the Boy Blue haystack has been sloped. Time: 10 hours plus 4 hours layout.

Fig. 16.9. Step 3—At midpoint. Note interrelation of various illustrations, and their locations to cut into framing slightly when needed, as on tree and pumpkin. Time: 30 hours.

Fig. 16.10. Step 4—Approaching completion with the "Old King Cole" tableau—quite a complex group. The lady in the basket was reduced from a full-page illustration. Time: 50 hours plus. Total time, about 60 hours.

tight curves, it is essential to use a gouge of appropriate curvature rather than a firmer. Bosting or grounding-out goes most easily with small flat gouges and a mallet (the latter to control length of stroke and prevent breakouts). Modelling can be done with the same tools, as appropriate for the particular area. I try to model accurately and cleanly so no sanding is necessary. This leaves crisp lines and good shadows.

The finish is the usual "antiquing," a couple of quick coats of satin-finish Krylon® varnish to inhibit stain absorption, then a coat of dark walnut Minwax®, immediately wiped off lightly to leave the darker color in cut lines and background. The final finish is to polish the Minwax®, then apply a coat or two of Kiwi® neutral shoe polish, which works better than furniture polish for me.

TYPICAL RACKHAM

"Samples" from "Mother Goose"

Hot Cross Buns...

Three Wise Men of Gotham...

Humpty Dumpty

Hush-a-bye; Baby

There Was an Old Woman

This Little Pig...

..to market   ...had roast beef   ..had none   ...cried "Wee, wee"

..stayed home

Fig. 16.11. Typical Rackham drawings which served as inspiration and patterns.

17

Two Nature-Study Panels

Fig. 17.1. Panel shows one bird and one animal (in whole or in part) for each letter of the alphabet, with necessary exceptions for X and Z. It could be done in various ways, but it is essential to keep the letters in order and to group associated figures as closely to the proper letter as possible to avoid confusion. Even so, and because of the lack of suitable (or desirable) birds and animals within the continental United States, it is only fair to provide viewers with a checking key.

Intended for a child's nursery, the children's room in a library, or even a classroom in school, this ABC panel is fun to design and carve. I made mine in imbuya and finished it in low gloss with no color, but it would take readily to painting with oils or acrylics. I find that it is very interesting not only to children learning their ABC's, but also to older children and even adults trying to identify the birds and animals through the letter clues.

You will note that I could find no animal or bird with a name starting with X, and only the zebra to grace the letter Z. Also, I have disregarded scale and used only the heads of some animals in the interest of gaining a compact panel. Incidentally, while I often design such a panel as I carve it, I would recommend advance design of the entire panel in this case, so you don't end up with an odd letter or two at the bottom. (My solution was to space four letters on each line and six on the bottom line, because of the absence of X and Z components.) I got my designs from a couple of bird guides and some animal books. The children's section of your local library can be a big help on this.

Of course it is not necessary to do the entire alphabet: This is a lengthy job; it took me about 60 hours and I carve rapidly. You may wish to make a smaller panel with one or more initials, each with its wildlife. You could make the grouping of favorite birds or animals in some overall shape of particular importance to the intended recipient of the carving. Some of

Fig. 17.2. Pattern for "Animal Alphabet" panel.

Fig. 17.3. This panel is unusual in that it attempts to include identifiable portraits of all the *distinctive* birds and animals of North Carolina. (It doesn't make sense to show all the warblers, sparrows, mice, and other multiple breeds which look essentially alike.)

Fig. 17.4. Pattern for "Nature Study" or "Aten" panel.

Key for Aten Panel

1. Work Horse
2. Domestic Cow
3. American Beaver
4. Collie Dog
5. Cat (or Lynx)
6. Domestic Pig
7. Mink (or Ermine)
8. Brown Bear
9. Woodchuck
10. Turkey
11. Chipmunk
12. Porcupine
13. Opossum
14–18. Baby 'Possums
19. Deer Mouse
20. Star Mole
21. House Rat
22. Red Fox
23. Flying Squirrel

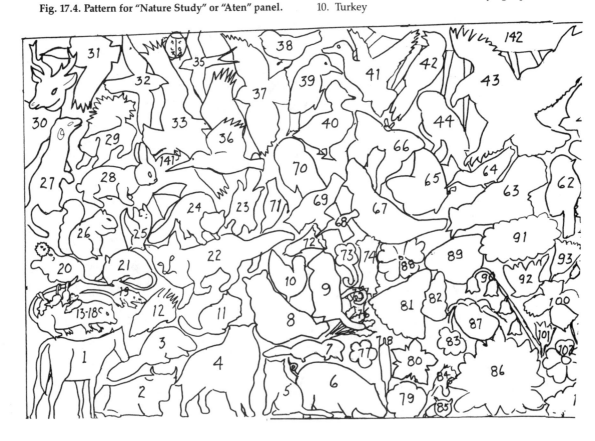

24. Raccoon
25. Bat
26. Gray Squirrel
27. Long-tail Weasel
28. Wild Rabbit
29. Striped Skunk
30. Deer
31. Night Heron
32. Chimney Swift
33. Osprey
34. Ladybug
35. Swallow-tail Kite
36. Pelican
37. Red-tail Hawk
38. Whippoorwill
39. Red-headed
    Woodpecker
40. Hooded Merganser
41. Blue-winged Teal
42. Magpie
43. American (Bald)
    Eagle
44. Barn Owl
45. Barn Swallow
46. Canvasback Duck
47. Bluebird
48. Mute Swan
49. Canada Goose
50. Purple Finch
51. Ring-necked
    Pheasant
52. Japanese Beetle
53. Goldfinch
54. Puffin

55. Belted Kingfisher
56. Snowy Egret
57. House Wren
58. House Fly
    (attacked)
59. Tiger Swallowtail
60. Robin
61. Chipping Sparrow
62. Brasstown Warbler
63. Blue Jay
64. Sandpiper
65. Monarch Butterfly
66. Luna Moth
67. Cardinal
68. Ruby-throated
    Hummingbird
69. Tufted Titmouse
70. Saw-whet Owl
71. Nuthatch
72. Morning Glory
73. Jewelweed
74. Wild Columbine
75. Jack-in-the-Pulpit
76. Blue Vervain
77. Buttercup
78. Cattail
79. Cow or Yellow
    Pond Lily
80. Wild Geranium
81. Purple Coneflower
82. Heliconia
83. White Violet
84. Arethuse or
    Indian Pink

85. Wild Ginger
86. White Water Lily
87. Yellow Lady's
    Slipper
88. Frangipani
89. Queen Anne's
    Lace
90. Lily of the Valley
91. Ox-eye Daisy
92. Bottle Gentian
93. Solitary Gentian
94. Dandelion
95. Lousewort
96. Black-eyed Susan
97. Pitcher Plant
98. Marsh Marigold
99. Hibiscus
100. Fringed Gentian
101. Bluebell
102. Wild Rose
103. Skunk Cabbage
104. Coral Trumpet
     (floweret)
105. Indian Pipe
106. Water Arum
107. Snapping Turtle
108. Terrapin or Land
     Turtle
109. Scallop
110. American Lobster
111. Periwinkle
112. Clam
113. Sea Horse
114. Bullfrog

115. Spring Peeper Frog
116. Archer Fish
     (attacking)
117. Angler Fish
118. Porgy
119. Angelfish
120. Carp
121. Bluegill or Sunfish
122. Fantail Goldfish
123. Yellow Perch
124. Atlantic Mackerel
125. Pompano
126. Cod
127. Sperm Whale
128. Porpoise or
     Dolphin
129. Starfish
130. Flounder
131. Grouper
132. Bullhead Catfish
133. Barracuda
134. Sole
135. Sailfish
136. Haddock
137. Large-mouth Bass
138. Rainbow Trout
139. Eel
140. Flying Gurnard
141. Brown Trout (in
     osprey claws at far
     left top)
142. Rim of the Sun—
     which enables
     them all to live

the subjects are, of course, from foreign countries because we are sparse in names to go with some letters.

The available imbuya was 11⅝ in. (295 mm) wide and I ended up with a panel 18¼ in. (455 mm) long. Thickness was a bit under 1 in. (25 mm). I allowed a little around the edges for self-framing, so the active area was slightly smaller. Also, I opened up the vertical spacing between lines from my original sketch, reproduced here. Background was cut down ¼ in. (6 mm). Carving was in two levels—⅛ in. (3 mm) and ¼ in. (6 mm)—to permit adequate separation of overlapping elements. The letters are at the lower level. Apparent depth was increased by darkening the background with dark walnut stain. Much of the setting-in was done with a ⅛ in. firmer and a small V-tool, with a shallow gouge to clear out the ground. However, I also used a ¼ in. firmer, with knife and ½ in. gouge for modelling. I provided most of the birds with perches, which adds some difficulty in carving feet but provides support; feet can be "designed off" if you prefer to avoid breakage. Some texturing of wing surfaces and bodies is advisable, to assist identification, and eyes are essential. I put in many eyes with a small drill, rotated by hand, others with a very small veiner. Where possible, I tied the letter in with the subjects as closely as I could, again for purposes of clarity. You will inevitably notice some design similarities in this book—I, too, have my favorites.

The ABC panel is, in a sense, a sort of introduction to a much more complex panel, the "All Things Beneath the Sun" or "Aten" panel. This is a polyglot of 142 mixed figures commissioned by a psychologist who wanted to use such a panel to instruct his son. (I should explain that "polyglot" is my term for a panel in which units are put in close proximity as in a jig-saw puzzle. There is no background; elements may be interlocked but unencumbered by branches, trees, brush and so on.) I tried to provide depictions of all of the local North Carolina animals, birds and flowers, plus some others I felt the child should learn to identify.

This is a very wide panel; it goes over a double doorway, so is difficult to picture, as well as explain, in the limited compass of these pages. However, the basic concept was, in my mind, "all things beneath the sun," which I think is a biblical quotation. The panel was 11¾ × 29¾ in. (298 × 759 mm) inside the frame. It was made in teak since it was to be placed near outside atmospheric effects. It includes 142 designs, any of which can be used individually. There are 31 mammals, 56 birds, 6 insects, 35 flowers, 4 amphibians, 6 crustaceans, 25 fishes—but *only one sun* (or "Aten," the Egyptian sun god). A very small portion of the sun is at the upper rim, and the flora and fauna are grouped in rays from it (see diagram). These seemed to me to be the proper selections for this commission; you may feel differently, in which case be my guest to change things!

This is, of course, an extremely complex panel to complete, but it is not particularly difficult. The main thing is to select distinctive poses when you can and not to duplicate look-alike animals or birds (assuming no color will be used for identification). Carving can be quite shallow if the background is antiqued. At first glance, a panel such as this appears to be crowded—and it is—but for educational purposes, it is hard to beat. But a panel complete with grasses, branches, or other terrestrial features can become too confusing and won't be nearly as informative for the subject in hand.

18

Try Christmas Mobiles

Here are some 75 patterns for carved animals and birds, plus another dozen Nativity and nostalgic figures. All were designed for double-faced flat silhouettes carved in low relief, but some became in-the-round carvings as I worked. Originally, I planned to use a variety of natural woods to get suitable tones, but I settled in large measure on holly. This decision led to another—to paint many of the units, particularly the birds, with oil pigments, a part of the job which my wife does better than I do. Also, it led to research for patterns in many different places, and choices in pose to suit the purpose. These things I will discuss in turn, but it is perhaps best to start by explaining the peculiar commission that caused all this.

The commission was from a frequent client, and by telephone as usual: "I'm tired of my conventional Christmas tree decora-

tions and want to do the tree all over—birds, animals, perhaps a crèche, a child with a sled, a cutter—and whatever else suggests itself to you. Let me know from time to time how you are doing."

In the first place, how many ornaments are needed for a tree? I asked friends, who always countered with a question (standard practice when you don't have an answer): "How big a tree?" Eventually I got around to a mean reply, "Give me numbers for small, medium, and large trees!" So nobody knew how many, what size, or the proper finish. I realized that anything large in-the-round would weigh down tree limbs too much, in fact that anything large would, so I set a size limit of approximately 4 in. (101 mm) for one dimension or another. The client's closing sentence was, "I want you to make the pieces of heirloom quality; I'm planning to divide them

Fig. 18.1. Ring-neck pheasant cock, chipmunk, bald eagle, osprey, monarch butterfly, and Polyphemus moth are all colorful and in action poses.

Fig. 18.2. Emperor penguin, barn owl, running horse, Saint Bernard dog, and the dove peace symbol make up this group. Horse and dove are untinted.

Fig. 18.3. These two birds, a chickadee and a hummingbird in flight, were tinted with oils and resulted in a request for tinting of all other birds and some animals. Tinting was with oil pigments in varnish.

Fig. 18.4. Rabbit, squirrel, and raccoon are in mahogany, with accents on coon tail and eyes. A slightly larger squirrel and a rabbit were made with bottom clips rather than screw-eye suspension, so they could sit on a branch.

Fig. 18.5. Two beagles, blue jay, downy woodpecker, and two dragonflies are all tinted. Dragonfly wings are clear plastic inserts, also slightly tinted green.

among my four sons." Perhaps basswood or pine or jelutong would be the easiest choice for the pieces, but holly is infinitely stronger and more suitable for detail. But it has one weakness of the softer woods in even greater measure—it is dead white. Holly is much harder to whittle, but the knife will leave a very good slight surface pattern and a soft glow to the wood. I did use mahogany where it was suitable unpainted—for the rabbit, squirrel, raccoon, and deer.

Bird and animal books, both adults' and children's, are sources of patterns. One problem with the usual compact bird guide is that all subjects tend to be shown perching, and I wanted no extraneous background. Also, the bird guide illustrator tends to follow a peculiar convention: He draws a side view of the bird to get in all major colors, but he actually twists the view just a little on top to show whether or not the tail is forked and how the wings come to rest. Also, photographs of animals and birds almost invariably include perspective, so that the far leg or legs is shorter than the near ones, a disaster for double-sided carving. Carved this way, such an animal looks deformed; you must adjust leg length so it is the same left and right, as it is on the animal itself. By consulting a number of sources (including dog and cat books and magazines), I got some variety in pose. Further, because the sources pictured their subjects in various sizes, I could use many directly and thus vary the size of my pieces—a desirable idea. Of course, it is impractical to consider scale, otherwise the mouse would disappear in proportion to the deer or bear, and the hummingbird and wren would be unseen in a group including the eagle. Further, I decided to show no backgrounds, no perches, and to carve the feet of larger birds when possible, equipping the others with legs made of four strands of twisted #24 copper wire, usually left unpainted.

All of the blanks except a few came from ¾ in. (10 mm) planks as planed, and in most cases were blanks less than half that thickness. I tried to select poses that

RABBIT   RACCOON

All figures are
5/16" silhouettes

POLAR BEAR w CUB

POLAR-BEAR CUB

CANADA GOOSE

GULL

HUMMINGBIRD
LADYBUG

CHICKADEE
MALLARD

MONARCH BUTTERFLY

BARN SWALLOW

ADÉLIE PENGUIN

RING-NECK   PHEASANT

POLYPHEMUS MOTH →

OSPREY

GRAY SQUIRREL

EMPEROR PENGUIN   ROBIN

BARN OWL   PAINTED TURTLE

Fig. 18.6. Patterns for Christmas mobiles.

Fig. 18.7. Robin, English bulldog, cardinal, white-tail deer, and two-headed turtles make up this group. Upper figures are holly, lower ones mahogany. The dog has faces on both sides, but the deer does not because of the horns.

Fig. 18.8. Beaver, squirrel (with clip instead of screw eye), normal turtle and fox. All four are mahogany, with tinted accents.

Fig. 18.9. Two bottle-nose dolphins and a crow. The crow is in ebony.

showed the animal or bird recognizably, some flying, running, or walking, as if the subject were quick-frozen in action. Almost all the figures showing a full face have the same full face on the back, so either side can be called the front and the ornament is free to rotate. This came about because I carved the raccoon (one of my first pieces) with his face at 90° to the axis of his body and gave him copper-wire whiskers, but all on one side. When the piece rotated, the back of his head looked just plain peculiar. The only later exceptions to the double-face rule were in-the-round pieces and the deer, whose horn location made a face on each side impractical. (On some others, the ear position is a bit tricky, but can be solved.)

It seemed logical to have some subjects seated on a limb rather than hanging: e.g., the squirrel and the rabbit. For such subjects, I bent a suitable clip of heavy iron wire and glued the twin ends in drilled holes. Most of the figures, however, are provided with small brass screw eyes at the proper balance point so that they can be hung with conventional hooks or with thread loops. However, some of the pieces (Star of Bethlehem, Holy Family, parasitic jaeger) were too thin where the screw eye should go, so I drilled them and provided monofilament nylon loops for hanging. In the case of the Nativity scene, I used silver screw eyes so the pieces could be used together more decoratively. Also, all of the Nativity figures have a flat bottom so they can be mounted on bases later if desired. One or two of the smaller birds, which would make attractive pendants if worn, I also provided with the silver screw eyes. One cat, the mouse, and the raccoon all have whiskers made with #24 copper wire glued in drilled holes, then trimmed and bent to the desired shape. One flight of fancy suitable for a pendant is the unicorn, who has a walrus-ivory single horn. One Magus also has an ivory sceptre.

Although my original intent was to limit myself to local birds and animals, it seemed logical to include a moth and a butterfly, as well as a sea horse. The client

GOLDFINCH

STARLING

BLUE BIRD

SPARROW

SPARROW

ROBIN (#2)

PAINTED BUNTING

CERULEAN WARBLER BAY-BR.

Bow

BULLDOG

PUP   ADULT→
BEAGLES

RETRIEVER

MOURNING DOVE

DOWNY WOODPECKER

KINGFISHER

RED-WINGED BLACKBIRD

DOBERMAN PINSCHER

Twisted wire

Wire whisker

HOUSE MOUSE

PUFFIN

PIPING PLOVER

PARASITIC JAEGER
(RED-BACKED) SANDPIPER

LEAST BITTERN

Seat surface

SIAMESE CAT

Notes:
Bird legs are 4 strands of
#24 copper wire, twisted.
Eyes are drilled holes.

Fig. 18.10. Patterns for Christmas mobiles.

Fig. 18.11. Sparrow (top), mourning dove, blue jay, and red-winged blackbird are all familiar on Long Island. Note screw-eye positions.

Fig. 18.12. Warbler (one of several carved), purple finch, nuthatch (note head is down), painted bunting, bluebird, black retriever, and another warbler.

Fig. 18.13. Baltimore oriole, house wren, screech owl, mallard, blue-winged teal, starling, barn swallow, goldfinch, and Adélie penguin.

Fig. 18.14. Left to right: Piping plover, parasitic jaeger, red-backed sandpiper, least bittern, and puffin—a group of familiar shore birds.

Fig. 18.15. Siamese cat (note branch clip), Doberman pinscher, unicorn (ivory horn), white mouse (copper whiskers), cat with ball, red-shouldered hawk.

Fig. 18.16. Swan with cygnet (note clip), boy on old sled (also with clip), and sea horse.

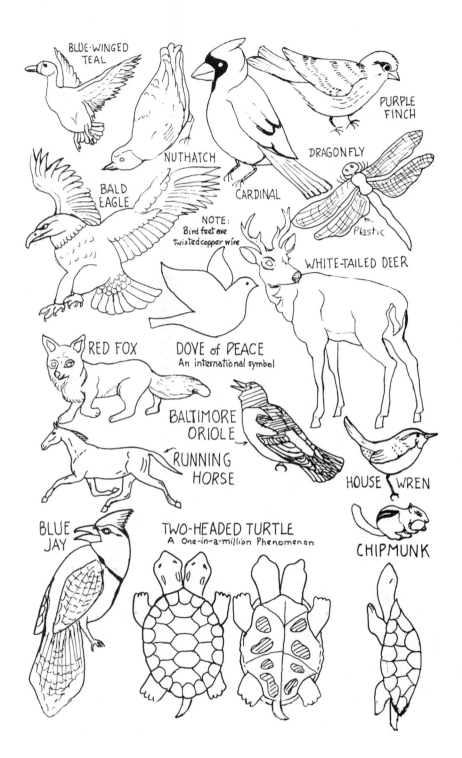

Fig. 18.17. Patterns for Christmas mobiles.

Fig. 18.18. Santa Claus has "fur" trim of glued-on sawdust, painted white. With him are two double-sided fake Fabergé Easter eggs, one gilded, the other painted.

Fig. 18.19. Angel choir, star of Bethlehem, and the Holy Family. The latter has wire halos and is hung on monofilament nylon going up from their crossing; the star also has a nylon hanger because of minimal top.

Fig. 18.20. The Three Wise Men, or Magi, are more or less traditional. Center magus has an ivory sceptre, and all have silver screw eyes and can be mounted on bases, as can other crêche units.

Fig. 18.21. Three shepherds, one a boy with an offering of wool. The men have crooks of bent wire painted dark brown; one carries a lamb, the other has two sheep at his feet.

Fig. 18.22. Cutter made from an old cigar box is black with gilt trim and swanshaped.

Fig. 18.23. A polar bear with cub, and a cub alone are in holly, unpainted. The mother and cub are on an ice floe.

Fig. 18.24. Patterns for Christmas mobiles.

The labels within the figure read:

HOLY FAMILY

Scene suspended from halo crossover will hang slightly askew

THE MAGI

ANGEL CHOIR

STAR of BETHLEHEM
Easier to carve w points are slightly blunted, viz:

OLD SLED

BOY w WOOL

SHEPHERDS

CUTTER (1-horse unit)
Body from cigar box w blocks to space

Reinforcing bar

Darker areas cross-hatched

Hitch bar

Heavy-gage wire

V-tooled scroll, gilded
Wood support legs

Double fins

"STANDING" DOLPHIN

RED-SHOULDERED HAWK

SWAN & CYGNET

CAT w BALL

requested a polar bear (so I made two) and the rare two-headed turtle (a freak of nature that occurs about once in a million among red-eared turtles—the client, who raises turtles, has two). The client also likes penguins. We could have gone on to less colorful local birds like the peewee, phoebe, and a number of shore birds, as well as such exotic and colorful ones as parrots, macaws, parakeets, and peacocks, or added local flowers. I mention these possibilities, because any one or several of these figures can be carved as pendants or single or multiple mobiles, thus getting year-round use rather than seasonal use.

There are also many nostalgic pieces like the little boy on the sled, the cat playing with the ball, the cutter (sleigh) with the proud lady and prouder Afghan hound. Here again, the multitude of "I remember when . . ." books and drawings will be helpful, not only for ideas but for actual patterns. My black-swan cutter was itself a modification from an etching of 1890 winter activities in Central Park, New York, and the lady's costume was modified from the same source. The cutter, incidentally, was carved from parts of an old Cuban cedar cigar-box, with seat lining of suede and runners of bent iron wire. With these figures, the client will probably use an earlier series of carvings showing skating, model skates, the history of skating, and the like. As mentioned earlier, any of these can be produced as individual pieces—I sold several copies of individual pieces to other, less affluent people who saw the work in progress. Most of these pieces can be produced complete in 2½ to 3 hours, particularly if a number of similar designs are blanked simultaneously.

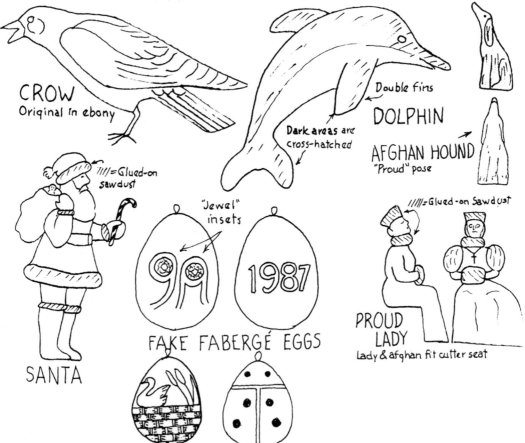

Fig. 18.25. Patterns for Christmas mobiles.

19

Small Religious Panels—Easy and Popular

Familiar major religious subjects take an enormous amount of time to carve, relatively speaking, thus are outside the spending range of the average churchgoer, even as gifts to friends. However, it is possible to make small panels that will be very much appreciated as gifts and can be sold at reasonable prices. Several such are shown here, including a Luther rose, the chalice of the Unitarian church, and a Jewish six-pointed Star of David containing the letter hi (pronounced "he," which is a

symbol of good luck and long life, among other things). All are done as reasonably small panels, none over a foot (305 mm) in any dimension. They can be hung on a wall or stood on a shelf. I did the rose and the chalice in walnut and the star in imbuya, so all look essentially the same. Also, all were carved in low relief, the chalice and star being merely deep incising while the rose is modelled and more elaborate. Thus the chalice and star can be carved rapidly by simply setting in and

Figs. 19.1 and 19.2. The Luther rose is a little-known but very attractive Christian symbol. It is somewhat more difficult, involving a nine-petalled flower with petals curving upward at the ends, so watch your step!

LUTHER ROSE

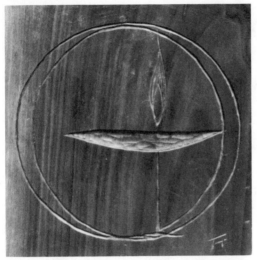

Figs. 19.3 to 19.6. Three forms of the Unitarian chalice, one including the dove of peace, and one as carved in walnut. The carving is in low relief with incising, and relies on textural differences for its effect. It is 9 in. (229 mm) square, with the carving stained darker than the background. The multiple-flame chalice cries for interpretation in marquetry.

grounding out. Some pigment (I used dark walnut stain) should be put in low areas to increase contrast. On such a piece, if the dark pigment runs over into the surface, it can simply be sanded or scraped away, but beware of slivers or small lines, because they will pick it up. An insurance method is to give the surface a coat or two of satin-finish spray varnish before staining; it will act as an inhibitor and also provide a base for polishing with Kiwi® neutral shoe polish.

Small crosses and bells are also popular religious symbols and are relatively easy to make in simplest form. Cross pendants can be the cross itself, either as one piece or with attached or inset arms (these may help cross-grain problems). An alternate is a circle, rectangle, keystone, heart, or other form with the cross appliquéd, carved, incised, or pierced on it. The cross itself can be carved, of course, and be of more elaborate form than a simple one— which should have the proportions of eight squares high and five squares wide (two each side of center), with the cross arm at the third square from the top. Latin crosses may be thinner than this, but not thicker. Many carvers add elements to crosses, such as floral ends or spear ends, inlaid wood or silver, variations in the simple shape such as undulations or notches, floral designs all over, and so on.

In addition to the basically simple designs, I have provided three challenging ones: the Luther rose, the choir duo, and the angel illustrating "Peace on Earth." Because the Luther rose has nine petals, I have provided a layout. It also has some tricky hollowing in the petals, so study the photograph before you start. The angel duo is highly stylized and interested me primarily because of the joining of the hands in an undercut loop away from the body, and the graceful treatment of the crossing wings—which are not the same on the two sides. The "Peace on Earth" angel, like all the others, can be a pendant with integral wings, or any size on up, of course—mine was 20½-in. (508-mm) tall because that suited the wood I had.

Figs. 19.7 and 19.8. The Jewish Star of David is actually two interlaced triangles, so you must watch in carving the crossovers. This one was carved about ¼ in. (6 mm) deep (although it appears to be appliquéd). The letter "hi" (pronounced "he") is in the center.

Flutes

Veiner line

Hollow this area

Alternate hemlines

PEACE on EARTH
Holly 12×20½″ o.a.

Figs. 19.9 to 19.11. "Peace on Earth" is in holly, 20½ in. (508 mm) tall and 12 in. (301 mm) wide. The wings are carved separately and attached, but can be integral. Note stylized face, but detailed hands—which seemed to be necessary to keep them from resembling mitts, as shown in the closeup of the initial carving stage.

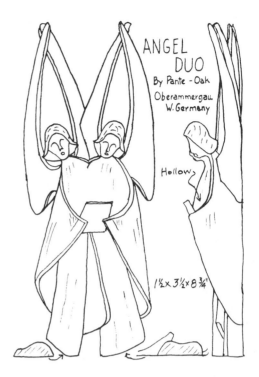

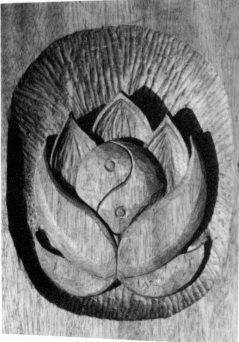

Figs. 19.12 and 19.13. The angel duo, pictured here in oak, is very stylized and involves removal of the wood between arms and bodies of the two. It is a challenge to carve but worth it. Note differences in wings from one to the other. This piece was carved in Oberammergau 25 or more years ago.

Fig. 19.14 (left). Not religious, particularly, but closely associated, is this personal logotype, carved in mahogany by my grandson for a client. The wood was about 2 in. (51 mm) thick, so he has trenched deeply to clear the lotus petals and round the central yin and yang to some degree. Personal cartographs, initials, coats of arms, and similar personal pieces can be produced—and sold.

20

A Relief to Win Literacy

One great virtue of relief carving is that it permits you to create a scene readily, which in-the-round carving does not, particularly if the scene involves such a thing as flying birds, or a total story with individual elements. This is not for the tyro, admittedly, but it is not difficult either because the pattern is clear.

The design is taken from an advertisement of the Give A Gift of Literacy Foundation, Minneapolis, for which bookstores and libraries were taking donations.

I began with a piece of imbuya (an import very close to walnut in characteristics) 12¾ × 14¼ in. (324 × 362 mm). I soon realized that a book in intaglio would be confusing at the very least, so I shifted to a relief book in a socket—very close trenching. Sockets are about ⅛ in. (3 mm) deep. This works out nicely to emphasize the emergence of the birds from the spaces between books. Further, the abutting upper spaces between books which are the bird silhouettes gave a natural horizon.

To further this result, I compressed each line of books until the horizon line had

Fig. 20.1. Give A Gift of Literacy Foundation uses this variant of M. C. Escher's "Sky & Water—I" to promote its work of collecting donations through bookstores and libraries to help the illiterate.

Figs. 20.2. Here the original drawing is converted to a three-dimensional conception. It is left with gouge marks to avoid a flat look.

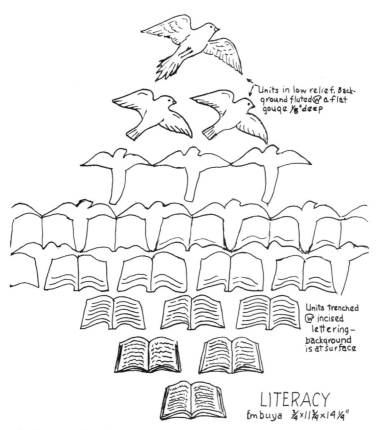

Units in low relief. Background fluted ⓦ a flat gouge ⅛"deep

Units trenched ⓦ incised lettering— background is at surface

LITERACY
Imbuya ¾×11¾×14¼"

Fig. 20.3. Pattern for literacy relief.

bird silhouettes wingtip to wingtip. Also, I enlarged the birds line by line somewhat so that the top bird stands out. The birds in turn move farther apart as they emerge.

The bottom book and the top bird are the only ones completely modelled; succeeding lines toward the center each show less detail as the number of units increases. The principal vehicles of detail reduction in the books were to cut the number of lines of "printing" and blur page edges, and on the birds to build modelling and feather definition step by step. The modelling was accentuated by "antiquing"—matte-varnishing the surface of the panel to inhibit stain soakup, then painting a dark walnut stain over the surface and wiping it off promptly to leave a darker color in the cut lines and base. However, because this piece of imbuya had developed an oxidized surface, I could, in effect, get three tones rather than the usual two.

When the sky was set-in, I left a flat-fluted surface of vertical lines irregularly spaced. However, the fresh wood beneath the surface was considerably lighter than the surface, so I left this unstained and later scraped the pages of the books as well to lighten them and remove traces of stain. I had originally intended to have the sky self-framed, but this seemed to pen the birds in, so the "frame" was removed to allow the sky to "bleed" off the panel edges.

It would appear logical to begin carving this panel at the centerline, defining the succeeding layers as carving progresses. However, it is probably better to do the uppermost bird (after setting-in) and the bottom book first, and to reduce the relative amount of detail line by line to the center where the importance of unit outlines must be subdued to create the effect of blending.

Part 3
Designs from
Around the World

21

As We See Ourselves

Every country once had its realistic native figures—unique carvings that came from nowhere else and depicted the natives of that country in costume at traditional pursuits. No more! Now we Americans have entered an era in which the depiction of the "natives" is done as caricature, usually not subtly. We have competitions to see who can carve the ugliest cowboy or Indian. Abroad, carvers in one country turn out in quantity designs that originate from somewhere else—because they sell. One result of all this is a sort of dreadful monotony. At shows, I have sought out designs that are different, that depict a bit of nostalgia, or heartache, or familiarity and are not slavish copies of a popular subject. Usually I fail to find them. I can understand a class of neophytes who copy a pet design of the instructor, probably working from blanks, but I can't understand skilled carvers content to turn out more and more of the same figure, year after year. Even Ford and General Motors change models.

In the so-called third world, much of the art is as traditional as our slavish copying of Gothic and folk pieces, and as subject to fads as our current interest in cowboy caricatures and decoys. But there the changes are made, the fads recognized, to scrape out a living. As foreigners visit and tour, or set up their businesses, the native art goes into decline as it has in Europe, and for the same reason. The woodcarvings that remain are tourist pieces—unoriginal copies of pieces that sell well.

To show what I mean by the rare imag-

Fig. 21.1. "La Malinche" was the mistress of Cortes and assisted him in his conquest of Mexico, so Mexicans are torn between admiration and disdain, just as they are about the Spanish conquerors. This figure of her was carved in Oaxaca and I bought it from a ridgepole on an adobe farmhouse. She is of copal, tinted, and about 15½ in. (394 mm) tall. Note the huge ears, elaborate headdress, but modern dress. She also had a slightly visible moustache, all indicative of the mixed sentiments of the youth who carved her.

Figs. 21.2 and 21.3. This caricatured couple, about 18 in. (450 mm) tall, were turned out overnight for me in Haiti. They are in primavera (a fake mahogany) and stained skin color. Their faces are amazingly accurate, although they are obviously caricatured. Note the "Masonic" emblem on the baseball hat—it is a voodoo symbol as well.

Figs. 21.4 and 21.5. Nicaraguan carving is quite primitive, as these figures show. They are in mahogany and about 5 in. (127 mm) tall, and are undertaking family tasks.

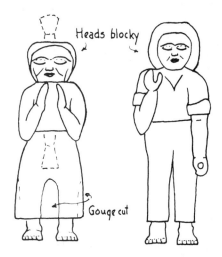

inative original, in this chapter (and all the last part of the book), I have included carvings from other lands that I think suggest the characteristics of their countries or origin and seemed to me different from what one sees day to day as tourist offerings.

Among remaining exceptions are the Trobriand Islands off New Guinea, where a Polynesian population has an almost unique art, passed on from father to son because there are no schools. The Maori in New Zealand, also Polynesian in origin, have set up a school to train woodcarvers in their unique art, and had trouble finding students, as did the European schools in Brienz and Oberammergau until recently. Bali, which is full of tourists and cheap carvings nowadays, still has some of the best woodcarvings presently produced. The Filipinos, like the Kenyans in Africa, are also very good carvers and are now producing carvings to be exported to Hawaii and Taiwan, or wherever else a quantity contract can be gotten, there to be sold as "native." North Sumatra Bataks are beginning to capitalize on tourism, but West Sumatra's Minangkabaus are still largely out of the tourist stream. Borneo, now called Kalimantan, is in the grip of exploiters of its wood and oil, but still produces good carvings in the interior. Ditto for Papua New Guinea and West Irian, the two parts of the island of New Guinea. India, Sri Lanka, Nepal and Kenya, and to a lesser extent Japan and China, have carving villages and "factories" still turning out their traditional specialties as well as some new designs aimed at the tourist markets—like netsukes and masks, for example. In our own area, Mexico, Guatemala, Costa Rica, Honduras, Peru, Ecuador, and Bolivia produce some excellent carvings.

Fig. 21.6 (left). Haiti has long been the source of sophisticated carving of its kind. I liked this mahogany head 15 in. (375 mm) tall. It emphasizes the Negroid features and is topped by a distinctive Haitian hairdo.

Fig. 21.7 (right). This bearded rebel 10 in. (254 mm) tall is from southern Mexico, hence in cedar and unpainted. His "uniform" identifies him and is reminiscent of Pancho Villa.

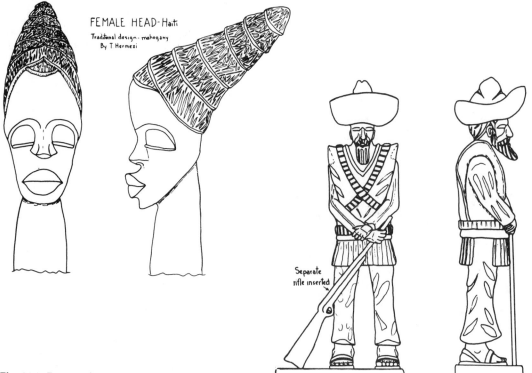

Fig. 21.8. Patterns for Haitian and Mexican rebel.

22

High-Relief Pointers from Spain

High-relief carving is less popular now than it was, but three present-day pieces from Spain revive the art and make some basic points. Spain is obsessed with the story of Don Quixote, and most tourists know the story as well, so it is to be expected that a high percentage of present-day Spanish carvings are of the Don in all sorts of sizes, poses, and garbs. There is little else new in carving there, but an occasional piece is surprising.

I found "Final Chapter" in Córdoba, a high-relief panel depicting Miguel de Cervantes writing at a desk, while over his head, as if it were what is going on in his mind, is Sancho Panza comforting the dying Don. This one is a scene within a scene, somewhat like a cartoonist's balloon showing what his subject is thinking or saying. But this is no cartoon; it does what 3D carving cannot—it combines two scenes in a single panel.

From the carving standpoint, this panel is also unusual in that it combines faces in profile, full front (almost) and at an angle. The profile is by far the easiest to do; a full face always introduces problems with the projecting nose, and the partially turned face adds the difficulties of maintaining proportion. Curves must be modified, made either more angular or more rounded. (Even the pro had trouble with Sancho Panza's face.)

"The Moneylender" presents a somewhat more conventional treatment of high relief (Figs. 22.1 and 22.2). It was produced in one of the best-known Spanish carving

"factories," Ouro. It is actually a combination of various relief thicknesses. The central figure and the bookshelves are in low relief, the shelves with the pottery in medium relief, and the outer figures in high relief. The medium-relief portion is level with the frame, while the outer figures project, as shown in the angular view, Fig. 22.2. The outer frame is ½ in. (12.7 mm) above the background, while the outer figures are about 1¼ in. (31.7 mm) above it.

Framing a carved panel can be a problem, and these two examples show different schools of thought. "Final Chapter" bleeds off the edges and is frameless, depending upon the background to provide contrast and frame it. (It is stained very dark.) Bleeding to the edges tends to suggest that the scene extends beyond the wood, but high-relief panels that bleed may look too thick. Here the carver has rounded the back of the 2-in. (5-cm) thick panel at top and bottom to get rid of any feeling of thickness or clumsiness. "The Moneylender" frame is much more conventional and has an enclosing or boxing effect that makes the shop appear small and confined or crowded.

In high-relief carving, the framing is always a problem, because the depth of the carving makes it necessary to use a correspondingly deep frame to hold the composition. This may create a shadow-box effect that puts part of the carving in shadow. Compare these framing methods: no frame, low frame, level frame, and box frame, and you'll tend to use the first two.

Figs. 22.1 and 22.2. "The Moneylender" is a carving-factory product from Spain. It is in chestnut, 1¾ × 9 × 15½ in. (45 × 220 × 390 mm), with a background that is ½ in. (12.7 mm) thick, and an integral frame 1 in. (25 mm) above the back.

I like in particular to use an idea from my amateur-theater days called "breaking the proscenium," in which the actors may enter the audience or be a part of it. This effect can be obtained in a carving by allowing parts of the framed design to project into or over a low frame.

High-relief carving requires a great deal of wood removal and usually is not speeded up by any attempt to rout out unwanted wood. Further, when larger gouges are used, there is constant danger of splitting or unwanted cutting, and the thicker wood is proportionately much more expensive. One way to get around this problem is to appliqué blocks of the same wood in areas which project above the general surface. These should be sawed to the general silhouette before being glued in place. It is of course essential to make sure that grain and wood color match. Location for such blocks can be determined accurately with a sketch on transparent vellum or a template. Another trick I learned from German ivory carvings is to carve a deep relief like a sandwich in a series of layers which are ultimately glued together in register. This makes it possible to carve a deer behind a tree or whatever. However, in larger-scale woodcarvings, the trick may not work—the finished layers may have to be separated by spacers. I had this problem when I carved "The Pied Piper of Mittenwald," described in an earlier book. I had the piper and several large rats on the pierced front panel, two sides of a Mittenwald medieval street for the second level, and a solid low-relief panel of the Alps and the Goethe church and house in the background. When I assembled them, I found they could not be laminated, but had to be spaced about 3 in. (76 mm) apart, and I had to make dozens of rats in high perspective on the "street" between them.

Fig. 22.3. Pattern for "The Moneylender."

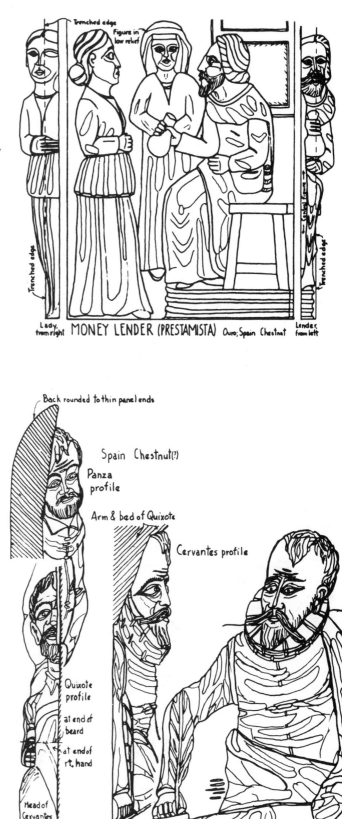

Figs. 22.4 and 22.5. "Final Chapter," a 2 × 9 × 23½-in. (50 × 220 × 350 mm) chestnut panel from Córdoba depicts Cervantes writing at his desk and thinking of the dying Don Quixote consoled by Sancho Panza (over his head). The carving is 1½ in. (38 mm) deep in some areas.

23

Haida—A Canadian West Coast Specialty

On the Queen Charlotte Islands, British Columbia, live the Haida Indians who, with some justification, consider themselves more creative and artistic than their neighbors. Early explorers brought back tales of the elaborate decorations on buildings and the totem poles and other objects carved by the Haida. The Haida seem to have a mild horror of duplicating designs exactly, and have enough imagination to change from carving to carving, and to adapt whatever they see as well as their own traditions to accomplish change.

When the explorers, whalers, and fur traders began to come frequently to the Northwest Coast at the beginning of the 19th Century, the Haida sold them sea otter and other furs until the fur-bearing population began to fail to meet the demand. Then they turned to carving items to sell, and the men signed on as seamen with some of the ships. Thus they saw

Fig. 23.1. These three pieces show some of the range of argillite carvings. The newest and largest depicts the killer whale Saoaa'io abducting Gunrah's wife, and is taken from a Haida tale. The central piece is a raven pendant, with abalone inlay in the eye, shoulder, and hip—probably a result of Maori influence. The pipe at right is an older piece of relatively simple design. It is 4¾ in. (32 mm) long, which suggests the sizes of the others.

Fig. 23.2. Two variants of the raven design, that at left in pine painted black, the other in coal. The wooden one has abalone inserts, à la Maori.

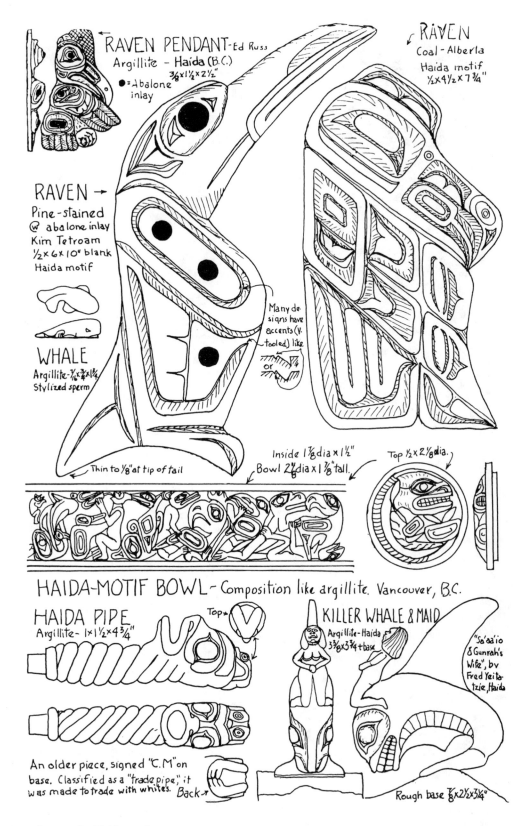

RAVEN PENDANT – Ed Russ
Argillite – Haida (B.C.)
⅜ × 1½ × 2½"
● = Abalone inlay

RAVEN
Coal – Alberta
Haida motif
½ × 4½ × 7¾"

RAVEN →
Pine-stained
w/ abalone inlay
Kim Tetroam
½ × 6 × 10" blank
Haida motif

WHALE
Argillite – ⅞6 × ¾ × 1¾"
Stylized sperm

Many designs have accents (V-tooled) like or

Thin to ⅛" at tip of tail

Inside 1⅞ dia × 1½"
Bowl 2¼ dia × 1⅞" tall.

Top ½ × 2⅛ dia.

HAIDA-MOTIF BOWL – Composition like argillite. Vancouver, B.C.

HAIDA PIPE
Argillite – 1 × 1½ × 4¾"

Top

An older piece, signed "C.M" on base. Classified as a "trade pipe," it was made to trade with whites. Back →

KILLER WHALE & MAID
Argillite – Haida
3⅜ × 3¾ + base

"Sa'aa'io & Gunrah's Wife", by Fred Yeitatzie, Haida

Rough base ⅞ × 2½ × 3¼"

Fig. 23.3. Patterns for Haida carvings.

HAIDA MASK
Original brooch in argil-
lite by Pat McGuire 4.9 x 3.5 cm.
(1.93 x 1.4 in.)

Figs. 23.4 to 23.7. These three pieces are all my copies of Haida designs—details are given in the sketches. The first two are large enough to be trays, while the mask is about 8 in. (203 mm) long, in teak.

other ethnic designs, Polynesian in particular, so their own carved heads began to sport protruding tongues and show other elements of Polynesian origin. They replaced the Maori paua shell with abalone and did very well. Most of their tools were handmade from bits of iron they traded for, or got as scrap off ships.

The other thing they learned was scrimshaw, which sailors in those days did to pass the time, giving their carved whale and walrus pieces to family and friends on their return to port. But the Haida added a twist—they had limited supplies of whale teeth and walrus tusks, and they made scrimshaw to sell, not to give away, so their livelihood was involved. They turned to a unique local material as an alternate to

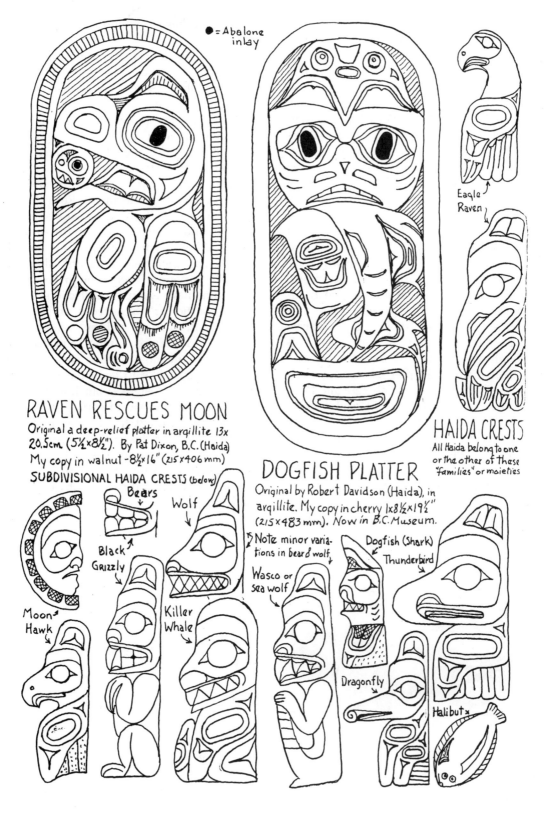

● = Abalone inlay

RAVEN RESCUES MOON

Original a deep-relief platter in argillite 13 x 20.5cm (5½ x 8½"). By Pat Dixon, B.C. (Haida) My copy in walnut - 8½ x 16" (215 x 406 mm)

SUBDIVISIONAL HAIDA CRESTS (below)

Bears

Wolf

Black

Grizzly

Moon Hawk

Killer Whale

DOGFISH PLATTER

Original by Robert Davidson (Haida), in argillite. My copy in cherry 1x8½x19½" (215 x 483 mm). Now in B.C. Museum.

Note minor variations in bear & wolf

Wasco or sea wolf

Dogfish (Shark)

Thunderbird

Dragonfly

Halibut

Eagle

Raven

HAIDA CRESTS

All Haida belong to one or the other of these "families" or moieties

Fig. 23.8. More patterns for Haida carvings.

ivory: a dark, almost black, slate of fine grain and without cleavage planes that carves almost like hard wood. This is called argillite and occurs in a mountain quarry just west of the town of Skidegat. It had been discovered by white miners at the beginning of the 1800's as an extension of their search for gold. So Skidegat became the center of a thriving argillite industry about 1820 and continued as the principal source until about 1880, when Massett, a town farther north on the island, became the second center. Many of the Haida in the two towns were related and some of their people had married into adjacent tribes, so they had a wealth of traditional myth to call upon for subjects, and they used them all. In addition to traditional pieces such as totem poles and totems and figures, they began to carve such European devices as pipes—although they didn't smoke themselves. Further, many of the pipes, as well as other objects, were really too elaborate and fragile to serve as anything but wall decorations. Museums all over the world now have these pieces, some depicting Europeans (particularly Russians, whom they saw coming down from Alaska), sailors, ships, and the like. Even in the 1820's, Haida carvers had far surpassed their sailor teachers, and continue to do so today. They have tremendous traditions to draw upon.

Thus it is that Haida argillite carvings have become true collector's items, particularly older pieces, and are nowadays quite expensive. I had seen and been shocked by the prices of some of these carvings as long as 20 years ago, but owned only one small whale until recently. In 1986, I was fortunate to find three pieces illustrated here, two in an obscure shop in Lake Louise and one in the Royal Canadian Museum in Toronto. I have also managed to find some literature on the subject, so could identify the carvers of my pieces. (There has been very little published on argillite carvings, even though so many museums have extensive collections.)

I am particularly attracted to argillite because of the variety of beautiful designs, the mythical origins of most, and because the carving in most cases is very shallow relief, which I like to do. I have recently carved several designs (I blush to say that they are straightforward copies) in wood, which are included here, as well as elements and other designs which may suggest something to you. These are tremendous exercises in texturing because of the shallow carving, and well worthy of study and emulation.

24

Canadian Carving

Canadian woodcarving has come a long way in recent years, as evidenced by the Canadian National Exhibition in Toronto, a huge fair that sponsors North America's biggest woodcarving show. I was therefore somewhat surprised to find almost no evidence of it during an extensive trip starting with the 1986 World's Fair in Vancouver, British Columbia, and extending across Canada to Toronto by rail. I realize that the same comments could be made by a traveler in the United States, because somehow or other, woodcarvings are just not generally in evidence. There as here, it was possible to find African and other cheap imports in malls and similar shops—usually at a discount indicating they were hard to sell. At the Fair, there was really only one booth that featured woodcarvings, and it was so crowded with familiar and hackneyed depictions of various wild animals that it was scarcely worth the time to examine it. Most of what I saw was not new in either design or execution, and the remaining saw marks and such were all too evident.

However, there were two sources of design ideas that were unexpected, one the Haida Indian carvings in argillite that were more-or-less duplicated in wood, described in Chapter 23, and the other the many miniatures shown in Chapter 8 carved in semi-precious stones or plain stones, all seemingly West Coast Canadian rather than East Coast. I also found a series of panels on birch done solely with pyrography that were excellent. Several of

Fig. 24.1. A pyrograph by Claude Gregoire of Ontario. It is a typical Ontario winter scene, 5 × 7½ in. (127 × 178 mm) on birch and done with a very fine needle so endless detail is produced, as might be done in drypoint etching. Note the melting snow with tree reflections, lines in road and snow, details on house, tinting of sky—all apparently done with the same needle.

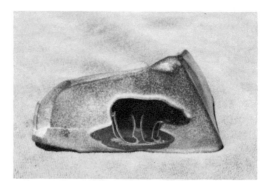

Fig. 24.2. A polar bear on an ice floe was carved into this rough block of green glass by a West Coast Indian. Because the bear is polished flat and his surroundings left rough, one can look through the bear to what appears to be the interior of his den—a fascinating effect. The bear is about 2 in. (51 mm) long.

the old and very familiar individual figures from Saint Pièrre-Port Joli were shown in specialty shops at very high prices, but none of the complex and different figures from that area were in evidence.

Another Canadian specialty which I have previously deplored seems to be increasing—that of reproducing good carvings in a plastic pressed medium. There were lots of imitation stone carvings produced by pressing a mixture of marble, limestone dust, and a plastic binder in a mold. And there were imitation coal sculptures made with coal dust and plastic, some of them of Haida designs and made to look like argillite. Some are even marked "Hand crafted," which the unwary will read as "hand carved"—which they are most certainly not. Their saving grace is that they *are* copies of good designs and that they sell for about a tenth the cost of the real thing, so the unwary tourist is not

too badly taken. (We have no reason to gloat. There are dozens of pieces of "native" art offered in Alaska that are the products of factories such as some in Seattle staffed by "Eskimos," or produced in Korea or Japan. Ditto for Hawaii, except that there some "native" pieces come from the Philippines.)

All is not lost, however. I did find some intriguing chair tops in a hotel dining room at Jasper, and very different kind of Welsh love spoon (authentic) in a shop near Toronto. There was also a good Indian head in Alberta, an interesting (although largely machine-made) grasshopper at the Vancouver Fair, and a very clever owl using the grain of sumac that reminded me of a bird I'd seen in New Mexico that I have added here. And the molded frogs and beaver were worth the price even if they were molded, because they can be done in wood.

Fig. 24.4. Miniature Canada goose is only about 1 in. long, but nicely shaped and an effective souvenir.

Fig. 24.3. Grasshopper is an assembly of various stained elements (see Fig. 24.8), really more woodworking than woodcarving, but cleverly done to utilize readily available wood sizes. It is about 8 in. (203 mm) long. The maker has several other insect designs.

Fig. 24.5. Indian head from Alberta is in cedar, stained, and almost 5 in. (127 mm) tall. The feather is left unstained. Note craggy face. With him is a clever stylized owl cut from sumac wood to utilize the bark and growth wood.

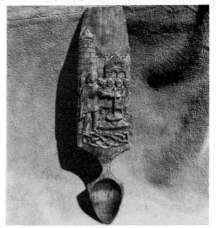

Fig. 24.6. This Welsh love spoon (an engagement token given by the young man to his fiancée) is quite different in design from any I've seen or made. It depicts the scene as Arthur pulls the sword from the anvil to prove his kingly heritage, and has an endless Celtic ribbon for trim. It is about 9¼ in. tall (235 mm), and has been imported to Canada.

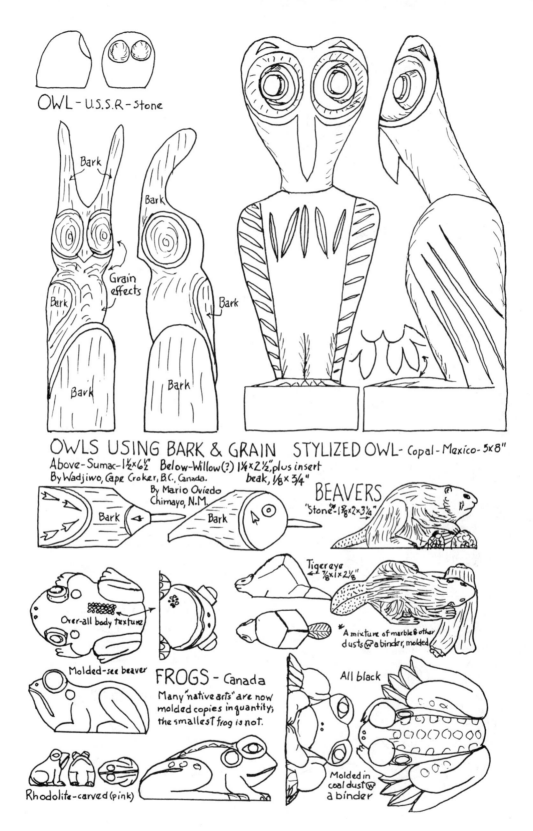

OWL – U.S.S.R – Stone

Bark

Bark

Grain effects

Bark

Bark

Bark

Bark

OWLS USING BARK & GRAIN   STYLIZED OWL – Copal – Mexico – 5x8"

Above – Sumac – 1½x6½   Below – Willow(?) 1¼x2½",plus insert

By Wadjiwo, Cape Croker, B.C., Canada.   beak, ⅛x¾"

By Mario Oviedo   BEAVERS

Chimayo, N.M.   "Stone"–1⅞x2x3¼"

Bark   Bark

Over-all body texture

Tiger eye ⅞x1x2⅛"

* A mixture of marble & other dusts @ a binder, molded

Molded–see beaver

FROGS – Canada

Many "native arts" are now molded copies in quantity; the smallest frog is not.

All black

Rhodolite – carved (pink)

Molded in coal dust @ a binder

Fig. 24.7. Patterns for Canadian carvings.

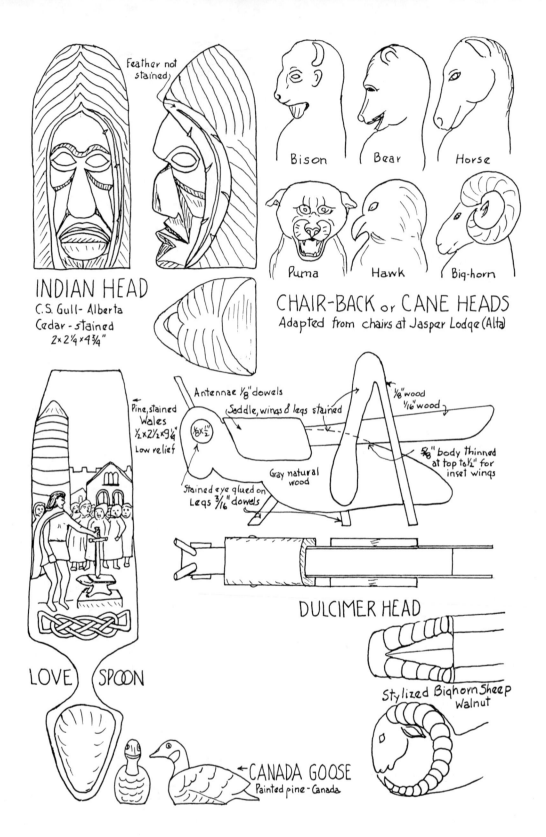

INDIAN HEAD
C.S. Gull - Alberta
Cedar - stained
2 × 2¼ × 4¾"

Feather not stained)

CHAIR-BACK or CANE HEADS
Adapted from chairs at Jasper Lodge (Alta)

Bison   Bear   Horse

Puma   Hawk   Big-horn

Antennae ⅛" dowels
Saddle, wings & legs stained
Pine, stained
Wales
½ × 2½ × 9¼"
Low relief
⅛ × ½"
Stained eye glued on
Gray natural wood
Legs 3/16" dowels
⅛" wood
1/16" wood
⅝" body thinned at top to ½" for inset wings

DULCIMER HEAD

Stylized Bighorn Sheep
Walnut

LOVE SPOON

CANADA GOOSE
Painted pine - Canada

Fig. 24.8. Patterns for Canadian carvings.

25

So—Carve an Egg

All of thirty years ago I found a small shop in lower Manhattan run by a Yugoslav whose daughter decorated Easter eggs in a way I had never seen. She was a student of the process, involving raw eggs ("to retain the soul"), wax, hot needles and a series of steps involving dye. I bought an egg and equipment for the process, plus color pictures, and my daughters enjoyed it. Several years ago, I toyed with copies of Fabergé eggs in wood for Christmas-tree decorations, but not until recently have I found a source of preturned wooden eggs. (I guess that is because this part of Long Island raises no chickens and darns no socks. Farmers used to use them to encourage hens to lay eggs.) The eggs my daughter found for me are of birch or maple, and slightly flattened on the bottom so they will stand on the big end. They are ideal for the present purpose, again a commission, to carve eggs depicting the Constitution, Santa Claus, and the Nativity.

A primary problem is to hold the egg during carving without reckless endangerment. One way is with a pair of small blocks hollowed to fit and holding the egg in a vise or by clamp if chisels are being used, or just by tape if it is being whittled—that at least keeps the ham of the holding hand a little farther from the cutting edge. This method permits fairly rapid resetting without damaging the surface of the egg by flattening it.

Designs are countless. There are simple geometric ones, flowers, vines, chip-carved patterns, weaving, and strap vari-

Fig. 25.1. The original Yugoslav Easter eggs, decorated with a wax and dye process in traditional motifs.

ations, such as I've sketched here. Beyond that are scenes, messages, portrait busts like the Ecuador Indians carve in tagua nuts—you name it. Finishes can vary from simple polishing, through staining, to tinting with oils. Mine are set on small stands for display, but they can also be hung as mobiles, light or shade pulls, and Christmas-tree decorations. At least, you can start with a blank that offers more than one possibility. You may have trouble finding the blanks, however. They're more likely to be in an art or decor store than a feed mill.

BERLIN EGGS - POLISH ORIGIN?

TRADITIONAL YUGOSLAV EASTER EGGS

Fig. 25.4. Traditional motifs for Easter eggs.

Figs. 25.2 and 25.3. Front and back views of my carved wooden eggs with designs representing Santa Claus, the Constitution, and the Nativity.

Fig. 25.5. An elaborate scene of mill and water (the mill wheel is detailed) carved by Kivel Weaver of Arkansas.

26

Ingenious Greek Folk Art

More than 2000 years ago, Grecian sculptors set the standard for classical sculpture that is still strongly influencing our art. But in Greece today, there is very little evidence of any striking modern production, from the evidence of tours and offers of shards and scraps of classical origin (or modern copies). However, the folk art of Greece is still strong and ingenious. I found a variety of designs, from realistic owls to stylized macaws, and from musical instruments to fish. Some have been shown in earlier books, but here are details of the more-ingenious ideas.

The fish nutcracker is unusual in its jointing, meticulous scaling, and the double socket to provide for two sizes of nut. The lyras are excellent examples of that rural art, chip carving, and have a general pattern that I saw duplicated in the Marquesas (see Chapter 28). But it's the jointed fish that have me baffled. All I can think is that somebody carved the fish, then sawed it apart, a section at a time, carrying on the double-hole drilling from piece to piece. I can visualize a longer bit that would drill from end to end, but I have trouble believing that anyone could know where such long drilling in wood would emerge, at least on an amateur basis.

Figs. 26.1 and 26.2. Nutcracker of olive wood closes to a fish shape. Note eye which is also a pivot, the scaling, flared handle, and double socket.

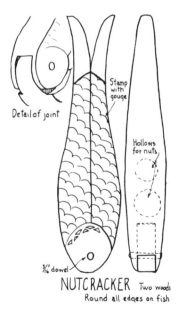

Detail of joint

Stamp with gouge

Hollows for nuts

3/16" dowel

NUTCRACKER Two woods
Round all edges on fish

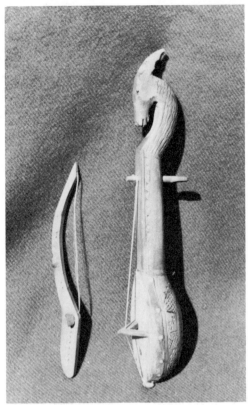

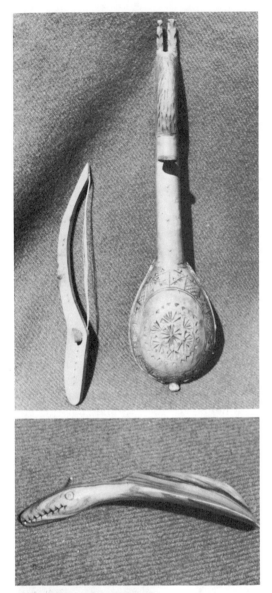

Figs. 26.3 and 26.4. The lyra has a sort of standard shape, with a horse motif at the top and copious chip carving on the bowl. It is one piece except for the peg, the belly being bored out from the front, then covered with a stretched-skin drumhead to form a soundbox. It is a single-stringed instrument.

Fig. 26.5. This olive-wood shoehorn is very utilitarian, with a toothed serpent head.

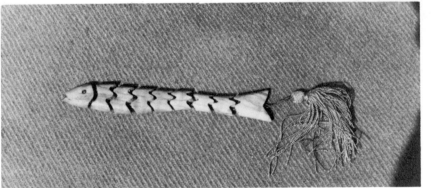

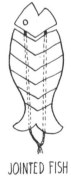

JOINTED FISH

Figs. 26.6 and 26.7. A typical jointed fish. This one is about 4 in. (102 mm) long, of olive wood, which is hard and unpredictable to drill. So how is it made?

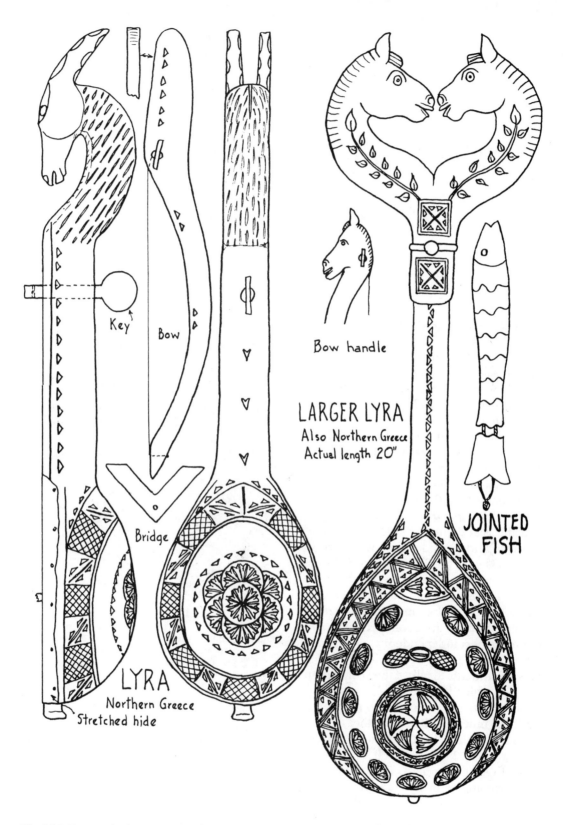

Key

Bow

Bridge

LYRA
Northern Greece
Stretched hide

Bow handle

LARGER LYRA
Also Northern Greece
Actual length 20"

JOINTED
FISH

Fig. 26.8. Patterns for lyra and jointed fish.

27

The Marquesas—Polynesian Carving's Birthplace

Alvaro de Mandaña discovered the Marquesas Islands in 1595 when he was on his way from Peru to the Solomons to set up a new Jerusalem. His patron was Don Garcia Hurtado de Mendoza, the viceroy of Peru, so he named them Las Marquesas de Mendoza, but only the first portion (which means simply "marquis") has stuck. They had, however, been discovered at least 1600 years earlier by canoe navigators coming from Indochina and China, probably by way of Samoa on the trade winds. In the interim, the first discoverers had populated the islands, established a culture of their own and carried it back westward to Samoa, Hawaii, the Trobriands (off Papua New Guinea) and even New Zealand (the Maori). The islands and landfalls were so widely spread and communication so infrequent that each developed its own culture rather independently. They still have a strong family resemblance, which leads art students to talk of the "Polynesian Triangle" which includes Easter Island.

The Marquesas lie in the south-central Pacific 780 miles (1,250 km) northeast of Tahiti, 2,500 miles (4,000 km) southeast of Hawaii, and 3,125 miles (5,000 km) west of the South American coast. They seem to be at the crossing of many trade routes, but the great circle tourist routes of the Pacific miss them completely, so they are not well known. Of the 11 islands in the group, all

Figs. 27.1. to 27.4. Tikis take many shapes, but with a common base. The big one is 4½ ft (1.4 m) tall and in a Swedish museum, the others are from Hiva Oa and are in miro wood and roughly 10 in. (254 mm) tall. Ancient stone tikis were blockier, with no separate legs.

volcanic, only six are inhabited, with a declining total population of 6,500. The islands produce only copra, coffee, and woodcarvings, most of the latter being sold to yachtsmen who pass by. In fact, the islands are so sparsely populated that only two have airports and docks. We went on the monthly freighter servicing them, the *Aranui*, and thus covered most of the in-

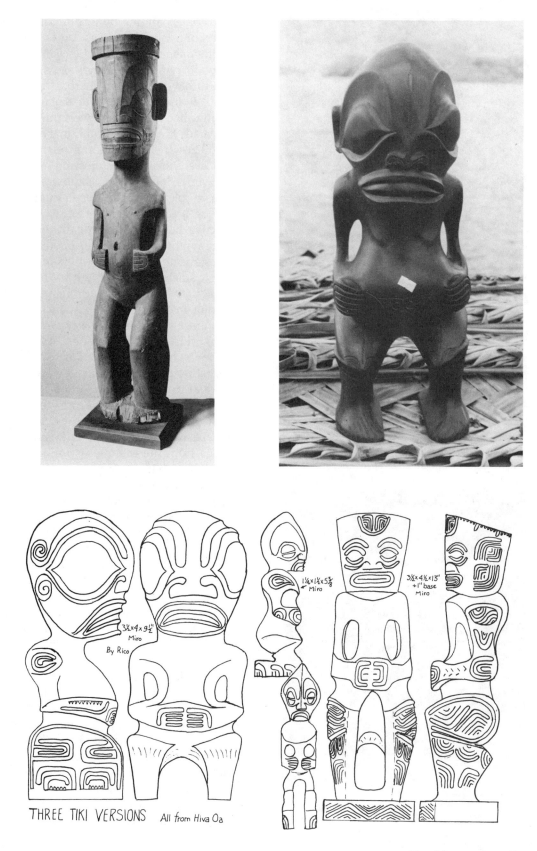

THREE TIKI VERSIONS   All from Hiva Oa

3¼ x 4 x 9½"
Miro
By Rico

1¼ x 1½ x 5⅞"
Miro

3½ x 4½ x 13"
+1" base
Miro

Figs. 27.5 and 27.6. The tiki is also a common architectural device. These are modern, one in front of the Tahara'a Hotel in Papeeté, and the others support pillars in the town hall at Hakahau, Ua Pou.

habited ones, landing by whaleboat to the accompaniment of bruises and bumps from the misnamed "Pacific" Ocean. All of the woodcarving of the Polynesians is supposed to have originated there. (I think it did, but it also died there, in a manner of speaking, because almost everything currently made is a copy of traditional designs and utilizes traditional design elements.) These are, however, interesting, strong, virile works, being done almost entirely with a couple of sizes of deep gouge. Patterns are arranged in very pleasing and distinctive but seemingly totally haphazard fashion on a given piece. There are no concessions to the tourist market except for a few small tikis. Pieces tend to be large and traditional in shape, with the variation occurring in the decoration, which often covers most of the surface, as is familiar in Indian, Sri Lankan, and Chinese work. All the work is in hardwoods and involves the chisel rather than the knife. However, the individual designs are so simple, yet so effective, that they deserve consideration. One would assume that the carvings would be widely exported. They are not; carvings from the Marquesas found even so close as Tahiti are of poor quality and even then relatively rare and very costly. The total population of Nuka Hiva, the largest island, is about 1,500, but there seems to be no central marketing operation—one must go from woodcarver to woodcarver out in the country to see what he has chosen to make recently. There are differences from carver to carver and island to island—one man being noted for tikis, another for war clubs, still another for bowls. But the best carver in the archipelago is Damien, who spends most of his time carving wooden elements for churches—pulpits, fonts, or Stations of the Cross, all immediately identifiable without signature. I was fortunate; when I visited his home there was a small ukulele for sale, far and away the best I've seen.

The other island notable for woodcarving is Hiva Oa with a population of about 1,000, and second to Nuka Hiva in size. It has the territorial woodcarving school, where young carvers are taught. (I bought two pieces by a 17-year-old who had only two months of training and already was doing enviably well.) Apprentices are seemingly taught to copy standard older works, so the occasional "sport" pieces like the fish tray pictured here are a rarity. It is obvious that students are allowed "freedom" within certain ironclad boundaries, so the variation between pieces is in motifs and their arrangement rather than in shape of the piece. And the pieces themselves tend to be traditional— ceremonial axes, bowls, hoes (!), war clubs, tikis, swords, daggers, tapa mashers, drums, and trumpets. There are no touristy giant salad forks and spoons, miniature god figures, and the like. But I was surprised to see that no two war clubs, drums, bowls, lances, or swords were exactly alike—the only duplication seemed to be in the standard round-headed tiki head, but from there on the carver seems to have adapted a series of dozens of basic patterns to fill a particular space.

Polynesian art in general tends to be monochrome and relies on form, as contrasted with Melanesian, which relies on color to attain its ends. The family resemblance between the work of the Marquesas and other Polynesian islands is today just that and little more; after all, each had the opportunity to develop over 700 isolated years. The missionaries arrived in 1797, and conversion to Christianity was so rapid that by 1818 the native religion and culture (and with it the woodcarving) were practically gone. Only under the influence of modern enlightened missionaries has it revived.

Tools were originally of volcanic stone, which would cut wood, mother of pearl, teeth, and bone. Even shark teeth were used as tools, and a hard stone was constantly at the carver's side so he could sharpen his tools. The adz was obviously used for bowls and big carving, the burin for details—these words referring to stone rather than metal. Polishing was done with pieces of coral or basalt, in successive stages of smoothness. With the modern re-

Fig. 27.7. Very rare in these islands is the mask, elsewhere so common. This one is, of course, a tiki variant.

Fig. 27.8. In the post office at Vaipaee, Ua Huka, is this magnificent chalice in miro wood. It should be in the museum next door! It is integral, with three tikis supporting the bowl, which has tikis for ears and two tiki faces. This is unusual in the Marquesas—an imaginative rather than a traditional piece.

Figs. 27.9 to 27.12. War clubs can vary in detail, yet all have roughly the same traditional shape. These are from varied sources on Nuka Hiva and Hiva Oa. The one held by the young lady is a particular prize, made by Damien. All are miro.

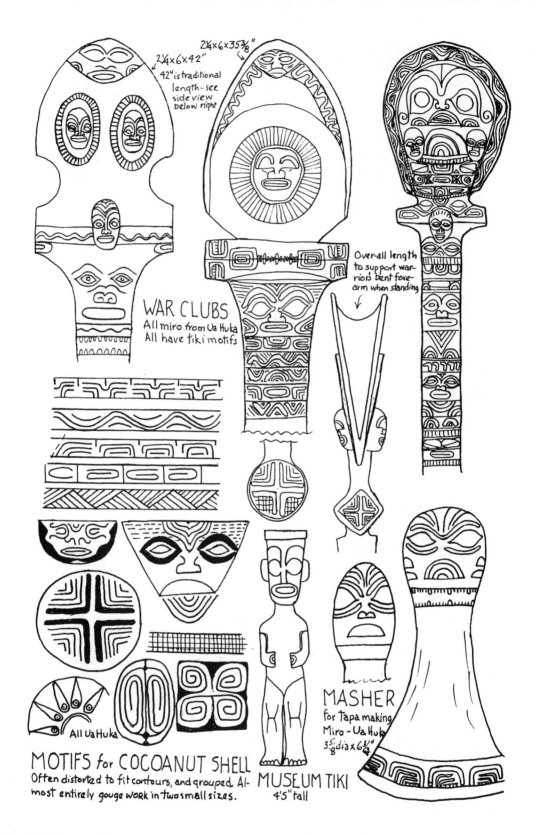

2¼×6×35⅞"

2¼×6×42"
42" is traditional
length - see
side view
below right

Over-all length
to support war-
rior's bent fore-
arm when standing
↓

WAR CLUBS
All miro from Ua Huka
All have tiki motifs

MOTIFS for COCOANUT SHELL
Often distorted to fit contours, and grouped. Almost entirely gouge work in two small sizes.

All Ua Huka

MUSEUM TIKI
4'5" tall

MASHER
for tapa making
Miro - Ua Huka
3⅝"dia × 6¼"

Fig. 27.13. Patterns for war clubs.

Figs. 27.14 to 27.17. The stone-toothed hoe is a ceremonial device rather than a weapon. Again, its shape varies within general limits. With one is a ukulele carved by Damien, a rarity, and with another a ceremonial sword, too delicate for actual use. Hoes are in miro wood, the sword in almond, from Atuona.

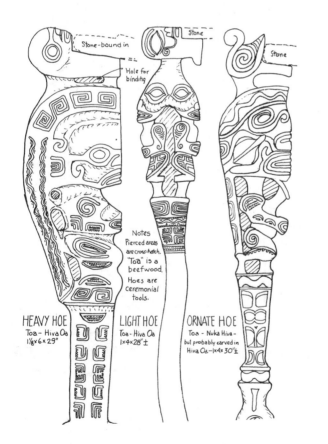

Stone-bound in

Stone

Stone

Hole for binding

Notes
Pierced areas are cross-hatch.
"Toa" is a beefwood.
Hoes are ceremonial tools.

HEAVY HOE
Toa - Hiva Oa
1⅛ × 6 × 29"

LIGHT HOE
Toa - Hiva Oa
1 × 4 × 28" ±

ORNATE HOE
Toa - Nuka Hiva -
bul probably carved in
Hiva Oa - 1 × 4 × 30" ±

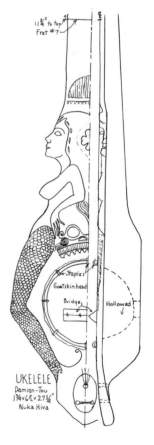

11¾" to top
Fret #7

Staples
Goatskin head
Bridge
Hollowed

UKELELE
Damien - Tou
1¾ × 6¾ × 27¾"
Nuka Hiva

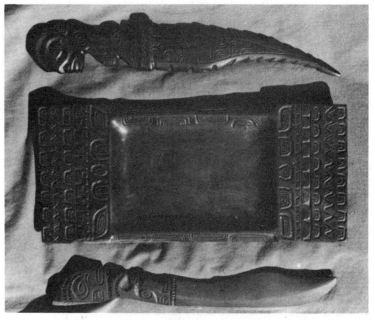

Fig. 27.18 (above). Two daggers from Nuka Hiva, one in tuo, one in miro, and a small platter in miro. The latter was made in the woodcarving school of Atuona, Nuka Hiva, by a relatively new student.

Fig. 27.19 (left). Two other ceremonial swords, the longer about 30 in. (762 mm). One has the back-to-back tikis also used for the heads of ceremonial paddles.

Fig. 27.20. Patterns for daggers and swords.

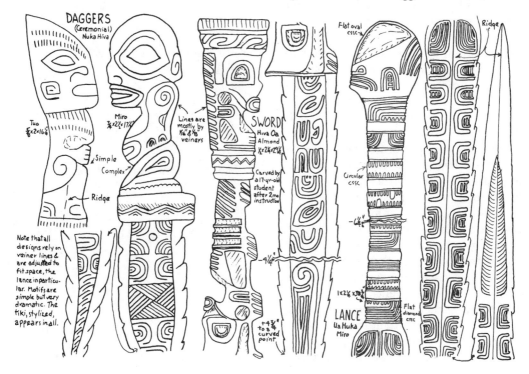

vival, of course, better metal tools are used, but each woodcarver still suffers from lack of an adequate number—probably the reason for the simple gouge motifs.

Woods include miro (Thespesia populinea), wrongly called a rosewood, for religious objects and ceremonial pieces; tamanu or átú (Colophyllum inophyllum), which I did not see in use; tou (Cordia subcardata), which is used for decorative objects such as ukuleles and statuettes; 'aito, called ironwood (casuarina equisetifolia) for furniture and weapons; and almond (not the edible-nut tree) used for practice pieces in the school only.

There are other woods, I'm certain, but these are the ones most common in local woodcarving. The almond is a light yellowy-tan and apparently like our nut woods in texture and hardness. Miro is a warm, dark-brown wood with black striations, somewhat like our dark-mahogany finishes. It is nearer a red than tou, which has about the color of our black walnut but with a more pronounced grain. Of the other woods listed, I have no direct knowledge because I saw no carvings made in them as far as I am aware.

Apparently, in the old civilization, and to some extent now in the new, the artisans, called tahu'a, were a high stratum, in most primitive societies considered to have a sort of special dispensation from the gods. The artisans were organized in fraternities by trade. Each fraternity had its own *maraé* (a stone platform, elevated, which served as a religious area), where suitable rites were performed before a new carving was begun. The carvers were men (and still are apparently). There is no question as one seeks one's way—everyone knows where each carver lives. Further, he does not bargain on price; it is considered degrading to bargain (thank the Lord!). If you attempt to bargain, they simply smile.

Workshops are at best very primitive—a thatched room with a bench or two and all hand tools. Usually no power—anything you get is assuredly handmade, and in daylight. Some of the pieces I have show tool slippages and the like, but were fin-

Fig. 27.21. The instructor at the woodcarving school in Atuona, Nuka Hiva, holds a plaque he'd just finished for presentation to a visiting French official. It is in miro and not totally traditional.

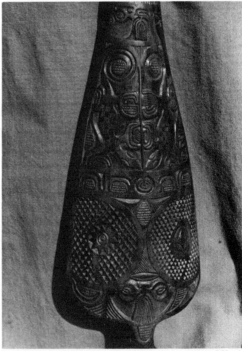

Fig. 27.22. Blade of a ceremonial canoe paddle in miro. It is from Nuka Hiva and 41¼ in. (1010 mm) long. Emphasis is on tiki variants, but spaces are filled with other symbols (see Fig. 27.23).

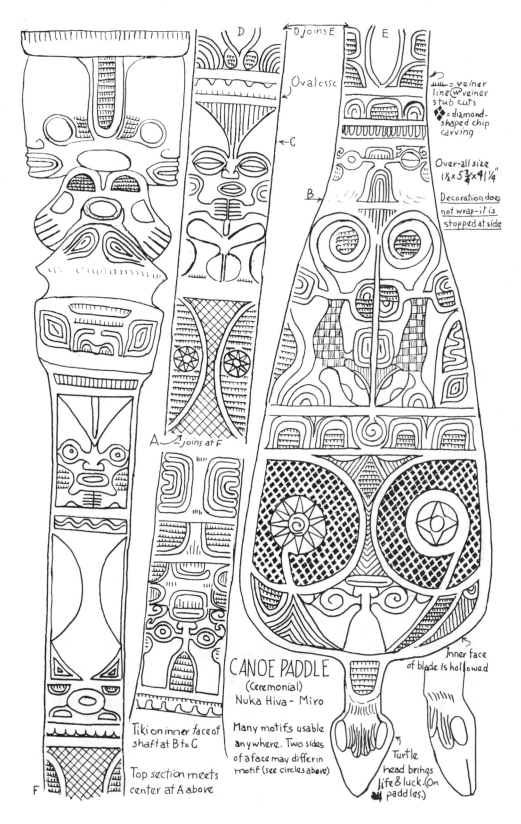

Labels within figure:

D

D joins E

E

Oval c s s c

←C

= veiner line (w veiner stub cuts

= diamond-shaped chip carving

Over-all size 1½ x 5¾ x 4¼"

Decoration does not wrap–it is stopped at side

B

A ↗ joins at F

Inner face of blade is hollowed

CANOE PADDLE
(Ceremonial)
Nuka Hiva – Miro

Many motifs usable anywhere. Two sides of a face may differ in motif (see circles above)

Turtle head brings life & luck. (On paddles.)

Tiki on inner face of shaft at B to C

Top section meets center at A above

F

Fig. 27.23. Patterns for canoe paddle.

ished anyway. (Nowadays, it is with sand-paper; once it was with pieces of coral or basalt of successively finer textures.) It amused me to recall the remark of an old American pro: "Make at least one mistake or the client will assume the piece was mass-produced!"

Characteristics of Marquesan carving that I mentioned earlier are interesting to examine in these photos and drawings. There is almost no evidence of use of a V-tool, upon which I rely. Gouge lines appear to be made by two veiners of about 1/16 (1.5 mm) and 1/8 in. (3 mm). There *are* larger gouges—I saw them on benches—but they are used apparently only in basic shape modelling. No color is added; no an-tiquing done—relief carving is done deeply enough so that this is unnecessary. The right-angled line with rounded corner is very common, but may be quite subtly carved; sometimes what appears offhand to be an arc ends short of its baseline or objective, and the one adjacent, starting at the base line or objective, is correspond-ingly short at the other end. (At first I thought this was carelessness, but it occurs too frequently and too regularly for that.)

The tiki is ever-present in the carver's mind; part of a tiki head, a complete head or even an entire tiki may be incorporated in a design, sometimes so intricately that it takes study to see it—but it's there, like a totem. Each carver seems to have in his mind also a set of standard motifs that he uses as needed to fill an area, but if none happens to fit, he'll invent one. And if the same space, reversed, appears on the op-posite side, he will not repeat his previous invention, but invent a new one. There is no absolute overall pattern or design on most pieces, two faces or two sides may disagree totally in proportions and motif arrangements, but they turn out as a har-monious whole. So much for our artificial rules, which inevitably lead to rigidity, stiffness, and dull uniformity. These carvers start out with a traditional overall shape and function, but they seem to have a very good time varying it as they go thereafter. They wouldn't understand our overall chip carving or diaper patterns, and what have you—which, admit it, do tend to become monotonous! In their own way, they're freer than we are.

Fig. 27.24 (right). A wooden trumpet featuring a tiki. It is now in a Swedish museum.

Fig. 27.25. A slit drum in miro with tuo stick, a long trencher, and a ceremonial sword, both in almond and carved at the school in Atuona, Hiva Oa. The drum is from Ua Huka. Compare elaborate sword carving with the simplicity of the more modern de-signs.

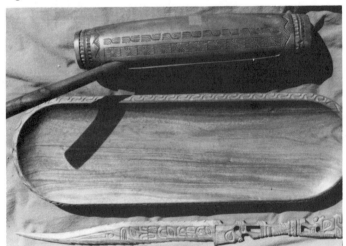

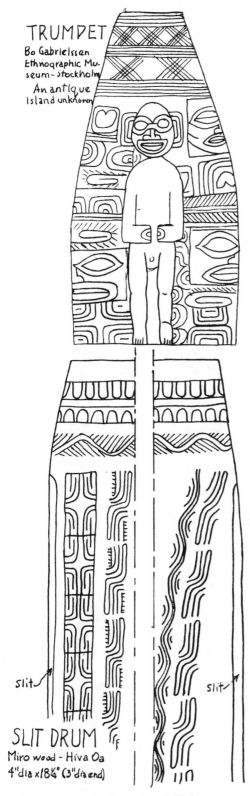

TRUMPET

Bo Gabrielssen
Ethnographic Mu-
seum-Stockholm

An antique
Island unknown

slit→

←slit

SLIT DRUM

Miro wood - Hiva Oa
4"dia x 18¼" (3"dia end)

Fig. 27.26. Patterns for trumpet and slit drum.

Figs. 27.27 and 27.28. The tiki in decoration can take many forms. These two are bedroom wall plaques at the Hotel Tahara'a in Papeeté.

Fig. 27.29. Churches in the Marquesas are often spectacular inside in terms of carved elements, and some are spectacular outside as well. This is the entrance to the church at Taihae, Nuka Hiva, all in carved wood.

Figs. 27.30 and 27.31. Two baptismal fonts by Damien, the stone one at Taihae.

Figs. 27.32 and 27.33. Two pulpits by Damien are quite different in style. The ship's prow has a complex natural base and is at Hakahau, Ua Pou. The eagle has a completely carved base with bullock and lion, all integral. The Polynesians are fond of floral garlands, and customarily bedeck their altars and figures with garlands to such an extent that some of my photos of those carvings were useless.

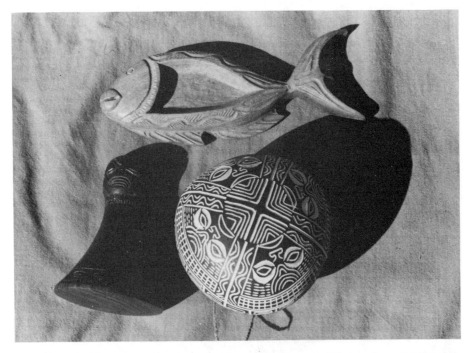

Figs. 27.34 and 27.35. The tapa masher is a ceremonial item. This one is in miro, from Ua Huka, and is 6¼ in. (152 mm) long. It is used to mash fibers from the banyan, mulberry, or breadfruit into a feltlike tapa cloth on which decorations are painted.

With it are a fish tray from the Hiva Oa school, carved by a 17-year-old student of two months. It is in almond. The third piece is a carved gourd bowl, reminiscent of the larger bowls for which islanders are famous.

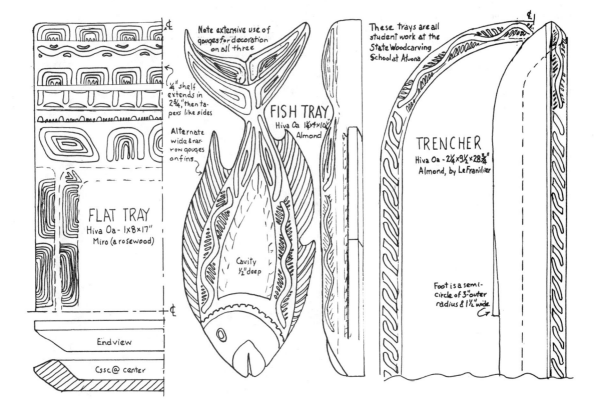

Note extensive use of gouges for decoration on all three

¼" shelf extends in 2¾," then tapers like sides

Alternate wide & narrow gouges on fins

FISH TRAY
Hiva Oa 1½×4×10½"
Almond

These trays are all student work at the State Woodcarving School at Atuona

TRENCHER
Hiva Oa - 2¼×9½×28¾"
Almond, by LeFranilier

FLAT TRAY
Hiva Oa - 1×8×17"
Miro (a rosewood)

Cavity ½" deep

Foot is a semicircle of 3" outer radius & 1½" wide

End view

Cssc @ center

Figs. 27.36 and 27.37. Two typical large food bowls. Every bowl has a different pattern and some can be 30 in. (762 mm) in diameter and cost more than $1,000.

Wedge motifs

Filler unit

Mixed motifs on a food bowl (A museum piece)
Designs are polyglot & unrelated in the 4 quarters.

Circular motifs

Tiki-head motifs as rim bands on otherwise-plain bowls

Polyglot-motif base - Jos. Vaatete
Vaapuiee Museum, Ua Huka

TYPICAL BOWL MOTIFS - mostly gouging

GAUGUIN SCULPTURE
Carved in the Marquesas Islands

SOYEZ MYSTERIEUSE

Left - Polychromed platter or tray (1892)
Center - Polychromed wood, like the piece at right from the "Soyez Mysterieuses 1901."

Fig. 27.38. Patterns for bowls.

28

Thai Carving Is a Blend

Thailand is an unusual country in that it has maintained its independence from colonialization. It is a constitutional monarchy that has undergone several shifts in emphasis since 1932, including a period of almost-democracy. Its 30-million-plus people are not all of one race. In the northeast are peoples closely akin to the Laotian tribes just across the border, and there is a large minority of Chinese. In the northwest, the people are closely akin to the northern tribes across the border in Burma, all of Chinese descent. The country is predominantly Buddhist, so there are literally thousands of heavily decorated

Buddhist temples and even more thousands of carved Buddhas in them. Some temples may contain as many as 500 carved Buddhas, and one contains a solid-gold 5½-ton Buddha that is estimated to be worth almost a billion dollars.

Modern Thailand is, however, between the legendary rock and a hard place as it has been for a century or more. It maintained its independence by a series of adroit maneuvers by its kings, but at some cost in accepting Western ideas. Despite the best efforts, Bangkok today differs very little from any other third-world capital influenced by the West. Its own mixed-origin

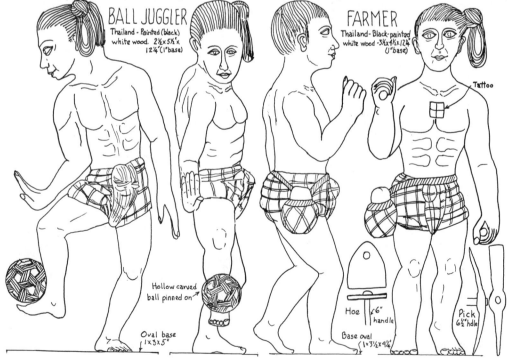

BALL JUGGLER
Thailand - Painted (black)
white wood. 2½x5½x
12¼"(1"base)

Hollow carved
ball pinned on

Oval base
1x3x5"

FARMER
Thailand - Black-painted
white wood -3½x4½x12¼
(1"base)

Tattoo

Hoe   6"
handle

Pick
6½"hdle

Base oval
1x3½x9¼

Figs. 28.1 to 28.5. Two muscular males beautifully executed, with plenty of anatomical detail showing movement. They are carved in a hard white wood and finished with black, suggesting ebony. They closely resemble Burmese work although they were carved in Chiang Mai; note the carefully done face, elaborate loin clout, hairdo. Ball juggling, incidentally, is a sort of dance, the hands executing classical poses while the ball is handled entirely with the feet and body, like a one-man soccer game. The ball is hollowed and separately carved.

Figs. 28.6 and 28.7. Folding-leg table is similar to those from India and Sri Lanka. Both parts are in teak, the interlocked legs being 15 in. (381 mm) long and opening out to a height of about 10 in. (254 mm).

The top can be lifted off as a tray 12 in. (306 mm) in diameter, so it has decorated edges. Various sizes and border designs are made, of course. The legs are a bit tricky to carve.

Fig. 28.8. Very modern lady is in teak and unusually tall and slender (4 × 20 in., or 92 × 508 mm). Her hands are in the classical greeting position, and she wears the longhi (like a sarong) and tall bun hairdo. Note the definitely Oriental face. Detail carving on the dress is very shallow.

peoples have their differing ideas and practices. Much of the commerce is in the hands of people of Chinese origin, which is common in the Far East. Its rich natural resources have been exploited by Western-based companies—also a common condition. It is currently engaged in a very extensive reforestation program to replace some of the teak that has been lumbered out. I saw teak planks 6 × 20 in. by 16 feet (150 × 500 × 4800 mm) in various places and endless rafts of teak lying in rivers for the year-long period of conditioning after cutting. Much of the wood construction is teak because of its resistance to insects, warpage, and rot, so the demand for it is always there, both internally and internationally.

The capital, Bangkok, which uninformed Western commentators have considered to be emblematic of the entire country, is not. It is a typical example of the modern capital, complete with skyscrapers and traffic jams. One guide told me that there are five million people in the capital and a million cars, because people commute from the suburbs there just as they do here, and there is no mass-transit system.

V-tool design on rim

Single-point punch

Back grooved 1" in from rim to receive triple legs

TABLE TOP or TRAY
Thailand - Teak - ¾" x 12" dia.

Figs. 28.9 and 28.10. Pattern for folding-leg table.

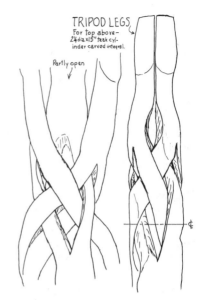

TRIPOD LEGS
For top above—24 dia. x 15" teak cylinder carved integral.

Partly open

HOSTESS - Thailand - Teak - 3½ x 4 x 20"

It is far different in the countryside. There trucks are gradually taking over from ox carts, and cars from carts and bicycles. This part of the country is rich with its traditions, some of which conflict with our Western ideas being imposed by economic pressures. Obviously, more and more of the traditions are being abandoned in the face of foreign involvements, and part of this is the abandonment of the strong and beautiful folk art.

Tradition plays a very important part in most Thai carving, and a lot of it is quite similar to that of Burma because the northern tribes of both countries are of Chinese origin (specifically Hunan) and are not particularly conscious of national borders between Burma, Thailand, and Laos. The people, and Burmese carvings, seem to pass back and forth between countries. Burmese carvings are imported or smuggled into Thailand and in such markets as Chiang Mai are common—and may be claimed by sellers to be Thai in origin when they are not.

There are also modern Thai carvings, some beautifully simple like the tall girl of Fig. 28.9. There is also a great deal of cabinet and box carving in relief, with motifs ranging from the vine-like scrollwork characteristic of Burmese carving, to floral and animal patterns. Many Thai carving shops produce boxes, chairs, tables, cabinets, and articles of furniture, mostly for export. In many such shops, the clerks are quite familiar with export problems and can quote times and prices for export, by various means of transport, to the United States. And there seems to be almost no black market like that of Burma.

Quite unique in Thailand is the employment of many women in woodcarving shops, not purely for finishing but for carving as well. We were astonished to see Thai women seated tailor-fashion atop cabinets on the floor, carving either the face or even the back panels! Many Western cabinetmakers these days waste very little time on cabinet backs or other not-too-visible details.

Because of the improved economy, there are a number of craft "factories" with some modern equipment, including electric power for basic machines. But most of the carving is still done in traditional fashion, with the work and carver on the floor. There are some tables for the carving of smaller pieces, but these are just tables without the holding devices we Westerners consider essential, and many of the smaller pieces are carved out in homes by individuals and only marketed through the factories or other middlemen. It is amusing, however, to note that in major carving centers like Chiang Mai as well as in shops in Bangkok, smaller carvings may be protected by careful coverings of transparent plastic wrap stretched taut in Western fashion.

There are many kinds of wood in this area, although teak is by far the most important. There seems to be little ebony left, in contrast to neighboring Burma, so other hardwoods are carved, then carefully painted black in imitation of ebony—just as is done in Africa. However, the carving itself in Thailand tends to be very carefully and expertly done, with much better cleaning up and finishing than is characteristic of African pieces. From small pieces to complete temples, there is endless detail in the work which can be extremely ornate. Teak is still the basic material for temple decoration, even though it

Fig. 28.11. Medium relief has been used in this circular panel of a jungle house. It is strongly stylized, yet somewhat primitive in treatment and is tinted to gain contrast between the natural teak and lighter and darker tones. The relief is about ½ in. (13 mm) deep, or half the thickness of the 12 in. (305 mm) panel.

Figs. 28.12 and 28.13. Quite sophisticated in contrast with the circular panel are these small rectangular ones of jungle and farm scenes. They are only ⅞ × 5¾ × 8 in. (23 × 149 × 203 mm) overall, with integral frames reducing the working area by almost 1½ in. (39 mm). The outer edge of the frame appears to have been molded on a jointer.

Fig. 28.14. Patterns for panels.

HIGH-RELIEF PANELS
Thailand - Teak - ⅞ x 5¾ x 8" o.a.
Carved area approx. ⅝ x 4½ x 6½"

Integral molding

MEDIUM-RELIEF DISK
Thailand Teak

⅞ x 12" dia.

Integral molding
Sea elevation ctr. left

Maximum carving depth ½"

Figs. 28.15 and 28.16. This is an elephant bell, and you can locate an elephant exactly in dense jungle because the sound carries for a mile or so whenever he moves a muscle. It is teak, with incised decorations of an elephant on the bell and floral sprays on the outside clappers, which are double-hinged.

Bore out 2¾"dia. x 4"
Saw slot

ELEPHANT BELL - Teak
Thailand   3¾ dia x 5¼"

Clapper-teak, tapered from ⅞ x 2½ x 5"

Hinge ¾ x 1 x 2⅜"
2 of each reqd.

Top 5-part design

may be heavily painted or gold-leafed or gilded. From what I was told, any other wood would have a very short life exposed to that humid and warm climate. The teak is usually treated with oil regularly if it is uncoated, however, something that Westerners forget to do.

I have tried here to present a cross-section of Thai carving art, ranging from the traditional and almost-primitive, to the modern and sophisticated. However, there is very little Thai art that can be called crude. Even hill-tribe (northern) art is quite well done and includes carvings of ivory, bone, horn, and other materials as well as wood. The carvers' knowledge of anatomy is exemplary, as evidenced by the ball juggler and the farmer. Their knowledge of perspective is shown in the relief panels. And their knowledge of design is obvious through all their work. There are many ideas here worthy of copying.

Fig. 28.17. A "tooth" with lion, a Buddha, heraldic lion, and elephant in ivory, and two orants (praying women) about 1¼ in. (32 mm) tall, of different woods—typical small temple souvenirs.

Figs. 28.18 and 28.19. Apparently, bamboo stems are crushed to make this two-part horoscope, because laminations are evident at the ends. It interested me, however, because of the excellent incised designs, obviously done like our scrimshaw—the design scratched in, then darkened with color. The only part of real importance is the script, which I can't read. You select the one for the day of the week on which you were born, and the maker has a book which tells the days year by year. (Both my wife and I were born on Thursday.) This kind of piece is sold at temple gates in some cities.

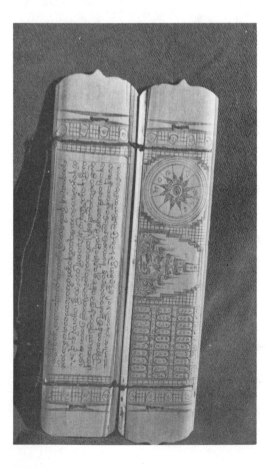

Figs. 28.20 to 28.23. Because teak resists humidity and rainy seasons, insects and warping, many Thai buildings have teak architectural elements. These are quite elaborate by our standards. Here are four examples: three sets of shutters, showing the framing as well, and the end of an eave on a temple. The eave, framing, and shingles are all teak, given occasional coats of teak oil. The shutters and framing are, however, brilliantly colored, and the figures are gold-leafed. And all this is exterior woodwork!

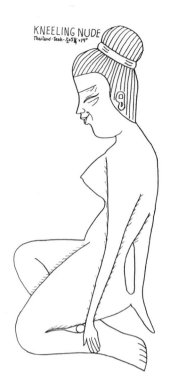

KNEELING NUDE
Thailand - Teak - ½ × 5⅞ × 19"

PEACOCK PIERCED PANEL
Thailand - Rosewood - ½ × 7⅞ × 25¾"

Figs. 28.24 and 28.25. Probably done for the tourist trade (although I saw only one), this nude is quite modern and stylized. She is in teak, ½ × 19 in. (12.7 × 483 mm). Detail is quite limited except for the face and hair.

Figs. 28.26 and 28.27. Rosewood is the material for this pierced panel of a peacock perched on bamboo. It is ½ × 7⅞ × 25¾ in. (13 × 200 × 656 mm) and basically very simple, but strong and decorative.

Figs. 28.28 to 28.30. These stylized pierced panels of mermaid and dancer have more of a traditional feeling. They are in teak, 16 in. (406 mm) tall, and are carefully textured including stamped designs on dresses. Note in each the characteristic careful hand positioning, particularly in the dancer.

MERMAID - Thailand - Teak - ⅝ × 7¼ × 16"

DANCER - Thailand - Teak - ⅝ × 7¼ × 16" - modelled

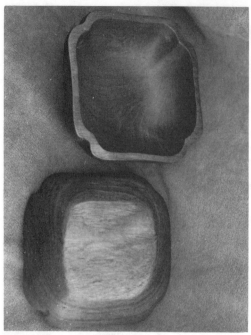

Fig. 28.31. Smaller teak bowls are probably an adaptation developed for the tourist trade, but very modern in design nonetheless. The sides, for example, are not straight but curve gracefully inward. It is 2¼ × 5¾ × 5¾ in. (30 × 146 × 146 mm), with walls ¼ in. (6 mm) thick, flaring out slightly at the top.

Fig. 28.32. Teak is the material of this graceful lotus bowl 3¼ × 9¼ in. (82 × 235 mm) in diameter. Its walls appear thin, but are really quite thick, as shown in the sketch cross-section. It was not turned on a lathe, but done entirely by hand.

Fig. 28.33. Traditional design of a temple-dancer bust forms the cap for this betel box of a toddy-palm nut, which is like a coconut but oval and only about 2¼ in. (57 mm) in overall dimensions. The wood looks like our oak.

Fig. 28.34. Obviously turned on a lathe, this 2¾ × 6¼-in. (70 × 158 mm) diameter tapered bowl is quite simple and easily carved in quantity. The simple floral design is cramped at the bottom to allow for taper.

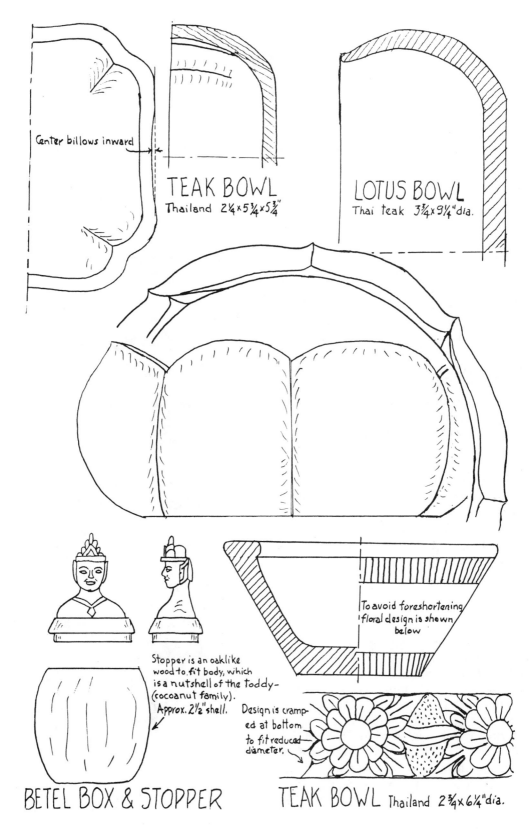

Center billows inward

TEAK BOWL
Thailand 2¼ x 5¾ x 5¾"

LOTUS BOWL
Thai teak 3¾ x 9¼" dia.

Stopper is an oaklike wood to fit body, which is a nutshell of the toddy-(cocoanut family). Approx. 2½" shell.

To avoid foreshortening floral design is shown below

Design is cramped at bottom to fit reduced diameter.

BETEL BOX & STOPPER

TEAK BOWL Thailand 2¾ x 6¼" dia.

Fig. 28.35. Patterns for betel bowl and teak bowls.

29

An Update on Bali

Bali is only one of more than 13,000 islands of Indonesia, and not the largest by any means, but it is better known to Americans than any of the others, and has been favorably compared with Eden by thousands of tourists. However, what continues to attract me there is the sophistication and beauty of its woodcarvings—even the tourist pieces turned out by the dozen—and the continuing development of new designs. I found four on my most recent visit (1987) although one was bought in a hotel shop in Medan, Sumatra. It was the devoted couple in Fig. 29.12. Two were new designs of bird reliefs, suitable for mobile or pendant, done in ⅛-in. (30 mm) macassar ebony, and the third deserves its own paragraph. I also was interested in comparing two more-or-less traditional masks, one in a wood with strong contrast between heart and growth wood, the other in macassar ebony. (The latter cost twice as much, but neither was expensive.) My interest lay in the fact that the "standard" design has been adapted by individual carvers until only a superficial likeness remains. I have tried to sketch the two side by side for direct comparison (Fig. 29.13).

The fourth piece was a prize because I've become a devotee of pierced or openwork carving, which originated in China. It is a cock-fancier feeding his bird. He has lifted the cage that normally keeps such birds from getting into premature fights and is feeding his prized possession from his hand. He is in typical male native costume, now unfortunately losing ground to shirt

Figs. 29.1 and 29.2. Compare these two masks, the darker in ebony, the other with much lighter growth wood. They are of the same good demon, but vary widely in detail (see Fig. 29.13), as carvers "interpret" the design.

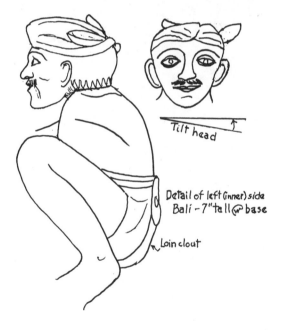

and slacks. But the fascinating element to me is that this carving is one piece of wood, despite the detailed cutting out of the rattan pattern of the basket (including the weaving) and the pattern of the cock's feathers. The cock's tail is jammed against the far side of the basket, and this is detailed as well.

I'd wanted for several visits to acquire some Balinese carving tools, but had encountered the practical answer of "first you go to the blacksmith and tell him what you want . . ." which is impossible for a visitor. This time I actually got five of the standard tools because the carvers from whom I bought them had duplicates to reduce sharpening frequency. Each carver usually uses about half a dozen tools, including five chisels and what they call a carving "knife," which is a spear-shaped piece of steel with both lobes of the spear point sharpened so it will carve either way. The other five are pictured. (Had I thought fast enough, I'd have acquired all six.) They are very interesting from our over-tooled standpoint. There are two chisels of $\frac{3}{32} \times \frac{3}{4} \times 10$-in. $(2.4 \times 19 \times 254$-mm)

Figs. 29.3 to 29.5. This unusual carving is only 7 in. (178 mm) tall but is one piece and very intricate in its detail. The cock fancier is feeding his bird, and holding the cover basket up to do so. (Cover baskets are essential or fighting cocks would fight each other to the death without an audience.) The feathers on the bird and every element of the basket mesh is depicted, including the crossovers of the weaving. The man is in traditional costume and beautifully carved as well.

tool steel, whacked out to order. The firmer is sharpened from only one side and the gouge is really nearer a bull-nose firmer, having a slight hollow ground in by the carver. Then there are two similar tools only ¼ in. (6 mm) wide and a jewel—a ⅟₁₆-in. (1.5-mm) veiner for the delicate jobs like hair and eyes. That's it—but you could shave with any. The knife, incidentally, usually has a handle, while the other tools do not. When needed, they are driven by a club or crude soft-wood hammer, not a mallet.

Four other Balinese pieces might interest you. They are antiques (there, as here, the term "antique" usually means about 30 years old, despite our law that sets minimum age at 100 years), extracted from a collection. They show delightful imagination and a real gift for caricature.

Fig. 29.6. These are typical Balinese carving tools, the usual full range. They are hand-ground from stock shaped by a local blacksmith. There are a wide and narrow firmer (sharpened from one side only), similar "gouges" made by grinding a curve into the flat stock and bullnosing the end. The prize is a very small veiner, also ground from the solid, for carving hair and eye details. These tools are supplemented by a "knife" with lobed-spear head, sharpened on both sides. It is the only tool that seems to need a handle.

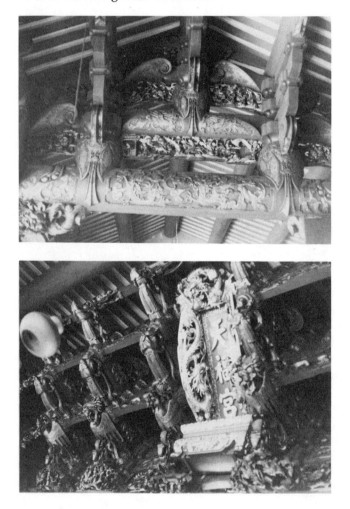

Figs. 29.7 and 29.8. Some idea of the ornate Chinese pierced carving that has influenced carvers in Burma and Bali, even Borneo, is suggested by these two views of the roof structure of an old Chinese temple in Singapore.

Fig. 29.9. The Balinese carve tree trunks with fanciful figures, but they usually invert them to get the root spread at the top. This is one of four flanking a court at the new Putri Bali Hotel.

Fig. 29.10. Doors in better buildings in Bali tend to be ornately carved. Here is a pair of narrow doors at Winnacottage Hotel, with a floral design.

Fig. 29.11. These delightful caricatures are "antiques" from a collection. Three are happy jokesters, while the fourth is a guardian warrior. The Balinese made similar figures, as well as realistic ones of common people, in their old temples, often of stone.

Fig. 29.12. The central figure, new to me, is an enjoyable fantasy. It is flanked by two familiar designs, a stylized owl and the yogi or "shy man," both in sandalwood.

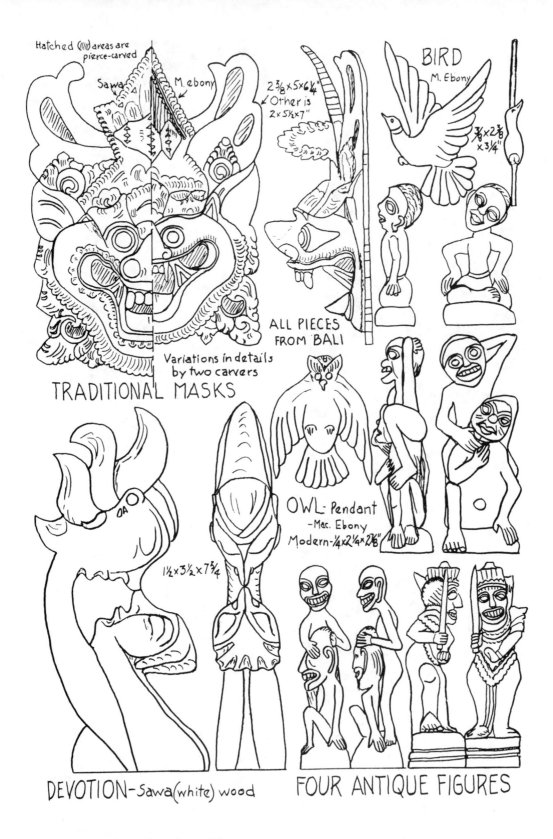

Hatched (||||) areas are pierce-carved

Sawa △ M. ebony

$2\frac{3}{8} \times 5 \times 6\frac{1}{4}''$ ← Other is $2 \times 5\frac{1}{2} \times 7''$

BIRD
M. Ebony

$\frac{7}{8} \times 2\frac{3}{8} \times 3\frac{1}{4}$

ALL PIECES FROM BALI

Variations in details by two carvers

TRADITIONAL MASKS

OWL- Pendant
- Mac. Ebony
Modern- $\frac{1}{4} \times 2\frac{1}{4} \times 2\frac{7}{8}''$

$1\frac{1}{2} \times 3\frac{1}{2} \times 7\frac{3}{4}$

DEVOTION - Sawa (white) wood

FOUR ANTIQUE FIGURES

Fig. 29.13. Patterns for masks and carved figures.

Figs. 29.14 and 29.15. Two new designs of birds for pendants or mobiles are in macassar ebony. They are simple and graceful, as compared with the painted crane at left.

Figs. 29.16 and 29.17. In macassar ebony, bracelets like this are also new. They have some variation in center boss, but are otherwise uniform.

All outer edges rounded

Alternate bosses

BRACELET – Bali – Macassar ebony – Size to fit.

30

Traditional Carving in Lombok

Lombok is an island just east of Bali and almost as large, but not nearly as well known. It has a population of about two million, more than half of them Moslem and the remainder largely Hindu like the Balinese—in fact they *were* Balinese who came over a couple of hundred years ago.

Because of the Balinese influence, and relatively little exploitation by the Dutch, Lombok has an overtone that is like Bali was before tourism became so pervasive. It is slower, quieter, cheaper, and about as beautiful. On a clear day, the central-island's active volcano Rinjani dominates from any point of view.

The economy is heavily agricultural and the best-known craft is weaving, but there is an active carving "industry" making painted wooden fruits, as well as more traditional items. I found a great number of very interesting "antique" pieces carved in horn, either bullock or cow, many designed as boxes with a great variety of motifs, some designs obviously based on the old animist religions that preceded both the Moslems and the Hindus and still hang on in the back country. Carving is quite competent and not done in quantity as it is in Bali, nor are pieces designed for the tourist. Efforts to start tourism there are moving slowly. However, the beaches are at least as good as those in Bali, and the surfing is said to be better, so the civilization in Lombok is changing and will continue to do so. Thus the variety of carvings may soon yield to sales pressures and we'll have some more elaborately carved giant salad sets.

Most of the pieces I bought there are of horn, but could just as easily be wood. They are largely boxes, but unusual ones include a circumcision tool. Note the variation in motifs. There is also a two-piece oil lamp, supposedly to hold enough oil to enable its user to read his Koran at night and in early morning. The wick comes up through the mouth of a seated frog, into which a metal tube has been inserted. I found the base for the lamp more interesting than the lamp itself.

Fig. 30.1. A masher or tamper for making tapa cloth is in a heavy wood and about 14 in. (356 mm) tall. It has a simple seated figure, and a quite conventional top-end design. The D-handle is reminiscent of the D-adz of the Northwest Coast Indians in America. With it are two peculiar antiques from Lombok, one a cake cutter with a roller that looks essentially like the old pie crimpers our sailors made in walrus ivory, and the other a fabulous bird forming the head of a comb. Both are in thin wood. (See Fig. 30.5 for patterns.)

In carved wood, the piece I was lucky to find is an elaborate holder for a plumb line. I understand that similar carriers are made in Korea and China but I failed to discover why. (We just have a simple metal reel, if that.) Another piece is a wedding box with narrowed waist. I was told that a newly married couple put their jewelry gifts in it. Sasak women wear a dark or black sari and sort of shirt, held in place by a matching scarf, and wear no gold jewelry. Such a scarf is suggested on the primitive female figure which shows the sari as well. Other wood pieces include a comb, a cake cutter (quite similar to American antiques) and a

rice cutter of bamboo. Some of the rice cutters are quite elaborately carved, the idea being to propitiate the rice god when rice is cut. The tendency is again to paint wood carvings black, except for the bamboo rice cutter and the plumbline reel, which is a dark wood, simply sanded and polished. It, incidentally, has high-relief figures of a frog, a lizard, and a crab, plus a man or monkey at the far end, all quite stylized. The rice cutter and the female figure are, however, from a megalithic back-country Sasak village, so don't exhibit the design or polish of the so-called antique pieces— "antique" here means at least 30 years old.

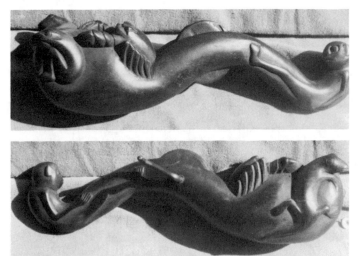

Figs. 30.2 and 30.3. A plumbline reel took on special form in old Lombok. This graceful holder is a one-piece carving featuring a lizard, a frog, and a crab at the large end, and a man or monkey figure on the handle. It is of a hard wood, smoothed and polished.

Fig. 30.4. Pattern for plumbline reel.

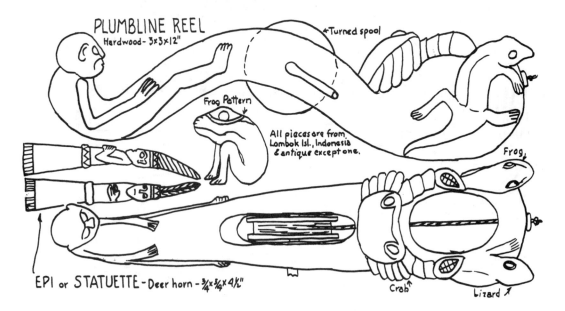

PLUMBLINE REEL
Hardwood- 3×3×12"

←Turned spool

Frog Pattern

All pieces are from Lombok Isl., Indonesia & antique except one.

Frog

EPI or STATUETTE-Deer horn-¾×¾×4½"

Crab

Lizard

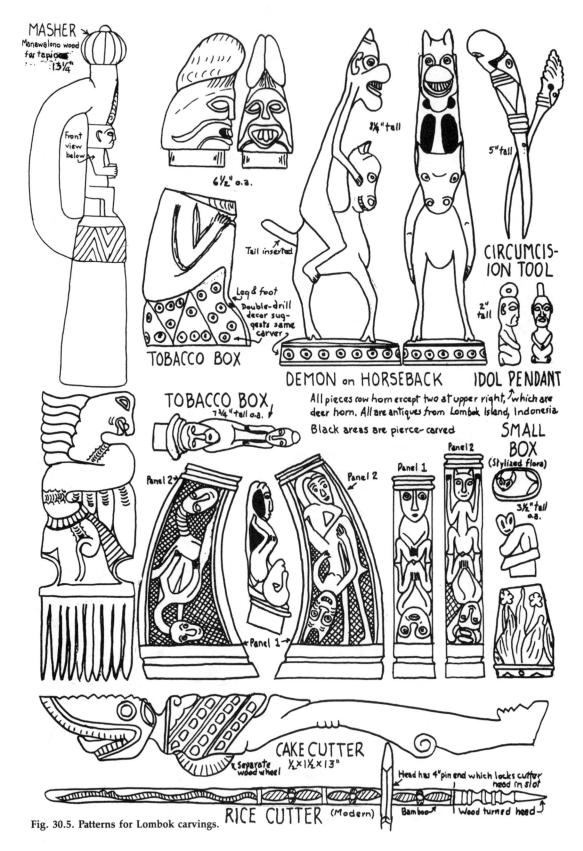

MASHER
Manawalono wood for tapioca
13¼"

Front view below

6½" o.a.

Tail inserted

Leg & foot
Double-drill decor suggests same carver

TOBACCO BOX

8¼" tall

5" tall

CIRCUMCIS-ION TOOL

2" tall

DEMON on HORSEBACK   IDOL PENDANT

TOBACCO BOX
7¾" tall o.a.

All pieces cow horn except two at upper right, which are deer horn. All are antiques from Lombok Island, Indonesia
Black areas are pierce-carved

SMALL BOX
(Stylized flora)

Panel 2

Panel 2

Panel 2

Panel 1

Panel 2

3½" tall a.a.

Panel 1

CAKE CUTTER ½ × 1½ × 13"

Separate wood wheel

Head has 4" pin end which locks cutter head in slot

RICE CUTTER (Modern)   Bamboo   Wood turned head

Fig. 30.5. Patterns for Lombok carvings.

Fig. 30.6. A primitive wooden female figure from a megalithic village contrasts with three sophisticated horn pieces, that at left being a grotesque human figure riding a horse, while the other two are boxes. One has a separate top with the ubiquitous frog and an incised design, while the other at first glance appears to be a solid figure, but it parts at mid-beard.

Fig. 30.7. Here is the opposite face of the frog-topped box of Fig. 30.6, and another box with more elaborate carving, including a pierce-carved (and top-heavy) stopper. Note the lugs at the sides of the frog box for a string by which to carry the box (probably for tobacco) and to hold the top as well.

Fig. 30.8. Here the reverse of the box in Fig. 30.7 dominates the picture. It is elaborately carved with mythical figures. At its left is a small horn box only 3½ in. (89 mm) tall, with incised side design and a carved dog on the stopper. On its right is a horn Koran study lamp, the stopper again a frog with a tube for the wick in its mouth. The body of the bottle is a simple spiral-carved piece, while the holder is an open basket with pierce-carved man, dog, horse and bush on it.

Fig. 30.9. The circumcision tool at left is horn, beautifully and intricately carved, and apparently strictly from Lombok; I haven't seen one anywhere else. With it are a duck in stone from Java, two unusual carved stones from Sumatra, as well as a miniature kris (dagger) and a carefully designed cased pick, also from Java, both primarily souvenirs. The two clam-shaped stones are old and pose somewhat of a mystery. They are covered with intricate cursive strokes extolling Mohammed, but the lettering is raised, not incised!

Metal tube for wick

6½" tall, o.a.

4¼" tall o.a.

Fluting

OIL LAMP & BASE – Horn

3¾" tall

3

3

2

1

WEDDING-JEWEL BOX

Wood, painted black

All pieces from Lombok Isl, Indonesia

FEMALE FIGURE

Wood – Modern 6¼" tall

All antique except

2

1

Carrying-cord lug

TOBACCO BOX

Horn - 5⅞" tall o.a.

Fig. 30.10. More patterns for Lombok carvings.

31

Headhunters Carved on Nias

Nias is an island southwest of Central Sumatra, 81 by 31 miles (130 × 50 km) totalling 1853 sq. miles (4,800 sq. km). It is important to woodcarvers in that a great deal of woodcarving was done there. It is important archaeologically as well, because of the series of megalithic (Stone Age) villages crowning mountain tops in the south, where the carving was done. The structures and culture there far surpassed those of similar areas in Sumba, Flores and Sulawesi (formerly the Celebes). The Niah inhabitants apparently originated in south China around 2000 BC and emigrated to

Nias via Assam in India. This accounts for the differences in culture, language, and carving style from that of larger and adjacent Sumatra. Further, the Niah rejected cultural change and were such good warriors that they defeated early Dutch attempts at colonialization (and seem to be resisting it again, because they have let roads deteriorate almost unbelievably in ten recent years of independence). Apparently the Niah were headhunters as recently as 1935, and are still renowned as fierce and courageous warriors. Even now, boys must jump three times over a stone

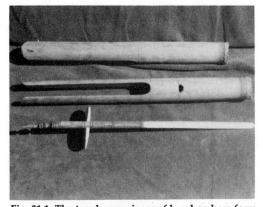

Fig. 31.1. The two larger pieces of bamboo here form a tuned pair of drums. They are beaten against a kneecap in a regular rhythm. Each one makes two separate notes, depending upon how it is held. Holding at the base produces one note, placing the thumb and one finger over the holes below the slot raises the pitch about three notes. With them is a rice-cutting tool from Lombok, also in bamboo, but elaborately decorated to pacify the rice god during cutting. The head and tip are separately carved pieces. This is from a megalithic village.

Fig. 31.2. This box, in afoa wood painted black, is a beautiful thing about 6¾ in. (176 mm) in diameter. It is carved from the cross-section of a tree, so I was certain it would check when removed from the high-humidity area where it was made. It checked as predicted—note the cover—but it is very interesting because it combines the Kalabulu and other designs on the top and has small panels of familiar objects on its sides (see Fig. 31.5).

column 6½ feet (2 m) tall to become men—this being the maximum height of the walls of enemy villages.

In the north of Nias, houses are family units on stilts, round and thatched. The culture that existed there was destroyed and artifacts stolen by early German missionaries. However, in the south, the houses are squarish, several stories tall on massive pillars, and are built cheek by jowl along an extremely wide court paved with stones. (The chief's house in one village has outside walls 52 feet (16 m) tall, and set on 3-ft (1-m) diameter pillars!) These villages are entered by wide flights of stone steps usually flanked with stone carvings, and can contain as many as 4,000 people. I found there a great variety of woodcarvings, particularly in one of the largest towns, Bawamatalua. The people are predominantly Christian now, so sell some of the animist and other pagan artifacts, as well as newly made ones. I bought one circular box knowing it would check, and it did by the time I got it home. The humidity is very high there, just under the Equa-tor, and this box had the fatal flaw of being carved *across* the trunk of a newly felled tree. But it is beautiful, and was inexpensive.

These villages, incidentally, still have the stone seats and vertical dolmens for ancestor worship, although in one village they had been draped with clothes to dry. And while the men now wear jeans and shirts like everybody else, they are still ready and willing to change into battle dress and do a series of war dances for the infrequent visitors—they did for three of us! (There was a time when the *Prinzendam* moored regularly offshore for day trips to the village of Bawamatalua, but tourists have been infrequent since that ship burned off Alaska. The nearest airport is 75 miles (120 km) away, so the village can only be reached by small boat at the mercy of the Indian Ocean or by Landrover, and either trip takes about six rough hours of rugged travel. But the trip was worth it to me, as the accompanying drawings and pictures attest. The pieces range from an extremely crude ancestral image of a

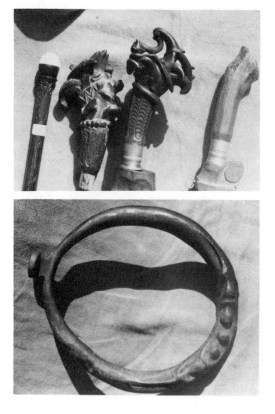

Fig. 31.3. Sword handles can be very intricately carved. The central two here have a superficial likeness but are quite different in design detail. The left one has a face resembling a clown, the right is a monkey design. A sword for daily use (in brush-cutting) is shown at right, with a handle that is merely shaped. With them at left is a baton that conceals an 8-in. dagger. It is from West Sumatra, and much more sophisticated in design and treatment.

Fig. 31.4. The Kalabulu is a large collar that will fit over a man's head and is worn loosely around the neck. It signifies that the man is a hunter and is considered to have mystic powers. It and a padded jerkin are essential to battledress. This one is all wood, but modern ones have a brass back and "button" and are not carved. Some older ones are carved all over with elaborate designs.

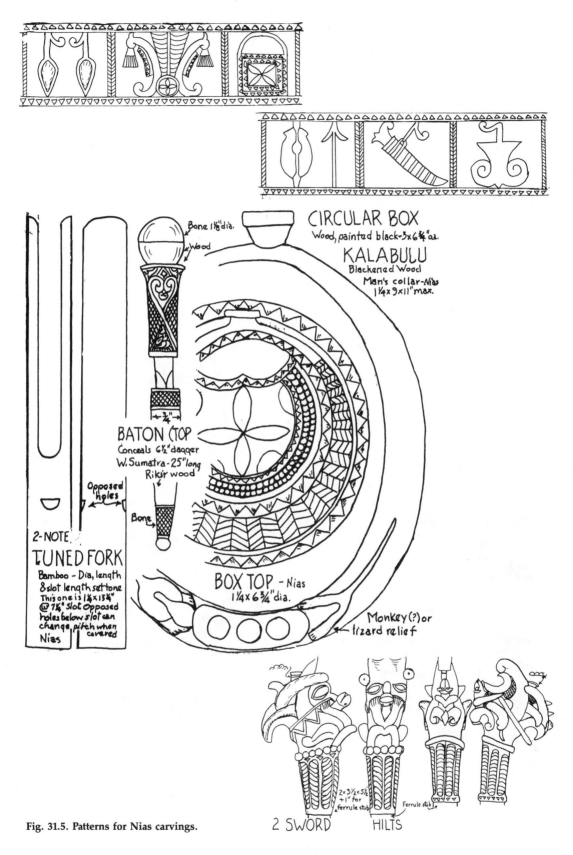

CIRCULAR BOX
Wood, painted black-3x6¾"aa.

KALABULU
Blackened Wood
Man's collar-Nias
1¼x9x11"max.

Bone 1⅛"dia.
Wood

BATON TOP
Conceals 6½"dagger
W. Sumatra-25"long
Rikit wood

Bone

←—¾"—→

Opposed holes

2-NOTE
TUNED FORK
Bamboo-Dia, length
8 slot length set tone
This one is 1⅝x13¼"
@ 7⅛" slot Opposed
holes below slot can
change pitch when
covered
Nias

BOX TOP – Nias
1¼ x 6¾"dia.

Monkey (?) or
← lizard relief

2×3½×5½
+1" for
ferrule stub

Ferrule stub

2 SWORD   HILTS

Fig. 31.5. Patterns for Nias carvings.

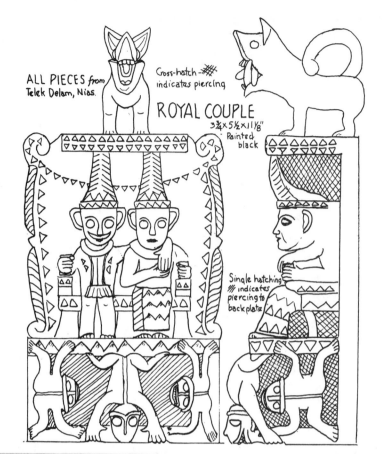

ALL PIECES *from* Telek Delam, Nias.

Cross-hatch ⧣ indicates piercing

ROYAL COUPLE
3¾ × 5½ × 1⅛"
Painted black

Single hatching /// indicates piercing to back plate

Figs. 31.6 to 31.8. There are relatively few carvers in Bawamatalua, but these two similar carvings of a royal couple were not made by the same man. Note the subtle differences in detail. Both are in soft wood, although the darker one has been stained black. It has the greater detail and greater accuracy, from background to such figures as the supporting monkeys and the guardian lion on top. It is primarily a wall decoration or sort of icon.

Figs. 31.9 a and b. Here is the warrior in all his finery. He has a shield, spear and a sword thrust through his belt—all carved separately. Note the elaborate headdress and the Kalabulu around his neck carved integral. The shield is set at an angle on a square plug where the left hand should be.

Fig. 31.10 (below). A miniature warrior is less elaborate than his full-size counterpart, but still has separate spear, sword, and shield. He is about 4 in. (102 mm) tall. With him are two ancestral figures, one in wood, the other in soft stone, and an elongated figure carved in deerhorn that is reminiscent of Batak work in nearby Sumatra.

FEMALE ANCESTRAL FIGURE - Telek Dalam.
Hard wood, painted black. 3¼ × 3¾ × 9' Very primitive

Hair is not defined on figures, but a hairdo is suggested here → Note large ears.

woman, to portraits of chiefs and their wives (women have a strong place in Niah life), elaborate sword handles, and boxes (including one with a small hand-carved balance with thinned coconut pans). The usual decoration is from elements of local life, such as the Kalabulu, a neck ring symbolizing skill as a hunter and also worn in battle. Handmade sword sheaths had a 4- or 5-in. (102- to 127-mm) ball of crab and bear claws just under the handle which I was told simulated Niah dominance of the world—a dubious explanation because I'm not certain they knew the world is round!

Most Niah pieces are 3D figures, carved in relatively soft afoa wood and painted black. However, the masher or tamper, which must be heavy, is in a wood called manawalonō, and at least one of the votive pieces involving the seated king and queen (or chieftain and wife), plus a guardian lion and three monkeys forming the throne base, is in a wood called gitō. The intricate sword handles are also in a hard dark wood to stand the stress on relatively thin sections. Note that the two I picture look alike at first glance, but differ in design details.

KING & QUEEN - Telek Dalam, Nias Isl., Indonesia
Soft wood, painted black.
King - 1¼ × 1¾ × 9¼" Queen - 1¼ × 1¾ × 8⅜"
Note - K = learring, Q = 2, all big. No other sex definition - he wears the apron!

Figs. 31.11 to 31.13. The crude ancestral figure of a lady at right contrasts sharply with the well-executed king and queen shown with it, yet all are from the same village. Note the head and neck decorations of the two figures and their uniform hand position, grasping a cup, as do all kings and queens carved here.

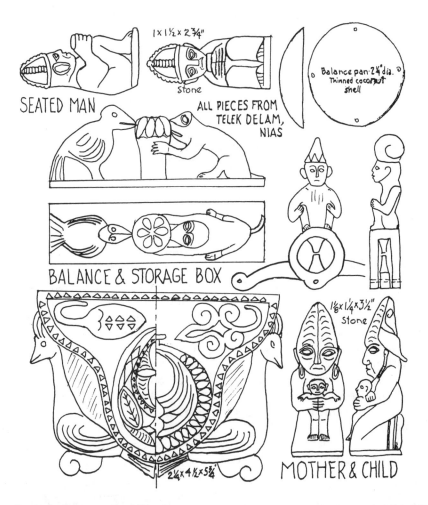

SEATED MAN

1 x 1½ x 2¾"
Stone

ALL PIECES FROM
TELEK DELAM,
NIAS

Balance pan 2¼" dia.
Thinned coconut
shell

BALANCE & STORAGE BOX

2¼ x 4½ x 5¾"

1⅛ x 1¼ x 3½"
Stone

MOTHER & CHILD

Figs. 31.14 to 31.16. The box at left is from Nias, that at right from Lombok; note the many differences. The left-hand box has on one face the Kalabulu worn by men and on the other the collar worn by women, with interspersed decoration. The top is inset and has a stylized bird eating, while stylized birds also form side handles. The Lombok piece (for sketch, see above) has a quite different but again unusual shape, with a crab on one face and two deer on the other, as well as an animal on top. I was told its primary function is to hold the jewels of a newly married couple, while the Nias box has inside it a miniature balance, beautifully carved and assembled. Scale pans are thin disks of coconut shell and beads provide decoration on supporting strings. Such a balance is used in Burma to weigh opium, but there is no opium here.

32

The Decorating Minangkabaus

The Minangkabau people of West Sumatra have a long tradition of decorating their longhouses, where a number of related families may live together, with elaborately carved and painted panels on vertical outside surfaces. Doors will also be quite elaborately carved, but are in fine woods and unpainted, although they have similar floral designs. Much of the carving is done in and around a town called Bukittinggi, particularly in a suburb named Pandai Sikat. This work and the houses are a bit florid by our standards. I was, however, so impressed by the prevalence of woodcarving there that I returned in 1987 for a second visit. (My first, four years earlier, was reported and illustrated in *Woodcarver's Pattern & Design Book*—Sterling Publishing Co., 1986.) I particularly had in mind getting a complete alphabet of the floral carved letters, as requested by some readers, and of attempting to get my hands on a rare local book of designs long enough to copy the guide prints. I was successful in both quests.

Herewith are a couple of pages of traditional Minangkabau designs, mostly for bands, from the book which contains more than 50. I have tried to select those which may be of interest to American carvers, and have added a few pictures of still other panels from which the designs can be taken as readily as from drawings. My preference is for unpainted panels, carved in a good wood to justify the carving time, but you can color them as brightly as you wish. The alphabets, used for signs, house numbers, names, and what have you, are usually painted as well, both to preserve the wood and to match the building on which they are mounted. Some of the small panels can be used for trays and shelf brackets, for example, or adapted for bedsteads and furniture. The most elaborate cradle I've ever seen (short of ornate royal ones in museums) is also pictured. It will sell for 450,000 rupiahs—about $280 American. Note that it is carved inside as well as out. It will *not* be painted but will be finished with stain and varnish.

Fig. 32.1. A traditional panel finished by darkening the background. Carving is fairly deep and wood is medium hard but stable under exposure.

Figs. 32.2 and 32.3. Front and wing of a traditional Minangkabau house shows the intricately carved and painted panels covering vertical surfaces of the building. Shutters and doors have their own designs as well. Some of the typical patterns are sketched (Figs. 32.18 and 32.19).

Figs. 32.4 to 32.7. These are typical Minangkabau doors, usually in teak which may be stained dark. They are usually highly polished and range in design from combinations of floral motifs to tropical scenes.

Fig. 32.8. Chip carving is incorporated in this circular table top, again carved with background darkened by stain—a tricky job.

Fig. 32.9. Top for a chair will be stained and varnished. Furniture is usually not painted.

Fig. 32.10. An oval tray is 13 in. (330 mm) long. No shaping has been done, so it could also function as a medallion ¾ in. (19 mm) thick.

Fig. 32.11. Oval design is 14 in. (356 mm) long. It features an unusual lotus.

Figs. 32.12 and 32.13. These two panels or brackets were made by the carver who lives in the house par-

tially pictured in Fig. 32.2. These are finished with stain and varnish, and are 9 in. (229 mm) long.

Fig. 32.14. The full alphabet and set of numbers extends the limited letters illustrated in *Woodcarver's Pattern & Design Book* (Sterling Publishing Co., 1986). These are slightly smaller than those previously shown (2½ in. or 64 mm)—as compared with 3 in. or 76 mm) in the earlier book, but thickness is the same—about 5/16 in. (80 mm). Pattern is a loose floral and spiral combination, varied to suit the needed shape. These are usually painted in several colors.

Fig. 32.15. This pair of brackets comes from Bukittinggi itself. They are 15 in. (381 mm) tall.

Figs. 32.16 and 32.17. I was fortunate to visit just at the time this elaborate cradle was nearing completion. It is carved both inside and out and set on a separate rocker frame. It will be finished with varnish and wax and will sell for 450,000 rupiahs—which translates into only $280 American.

TRADITIONAL MINANGKABAU
DESIGNS *for* RELIEF PANELS – I

Selected from a Museum collection in Bukittinggi,
W. Sumatra. These panels, brightly painted in colors,
can cover the entire façade of the unique house.

Angled corners

Moldings or edgings

Fig. 32.18. Patterns for relief panels.

Fig. 32.19. More patterns for relief panels.

33

Horn, Shell, Bone, Stone, Gourd, and Tagua

Whittling can very well be described as a disease, because it strikes the afflicted whether or not they have wood to whittle. In Chile, where there is very little wood, I found that Indians carved whale teeth, as they do in the Azores and elsewhere. In Italy, a whole industry has existed for years around carved shell, most of it the familiar cameo. There are carved olive pits from China and carved coconut shells from the South Pacific. My grandfather taught me how to make a basket of a peachstone. I've seen carved cherry and apricot pits here, avocado pits in Israel, horn in South American, Asia and Africa, various nuts in Papua New Guinea—so the disease must be universal.

Obviously, many of the designs carved into other materials can be carved in wood as well, although I'd hate to try transferring the Burmese lyre player (Illus. 33.1) from shell to wood, for example. And my experience with bone, crocodile teeth, gourd, coconut shell, horn, ivory, and shell leave me totally unsatisfied and totally admiring of the pieces I've seen. I've tried them all, and I bow to better men.

However, many of the pieces I've sketched and photographed in this group can be done, and with no more than a pocketknife or a couple of good carving tools. I've done them, and discovered a new way to be frustrated. So I pass it on.

You may have the necessary steadier hand, patience, time, and skill that it takes. Never underestimate these pieces, or think they are done by unskilled labor! And don't brag when you copy one in wood—even if it is the same size. You have tools which the carvers of most of these pieces do not.

Fig. 33.1. Shell can be carved into very delicate designs. Witness this Burmese harpist in which the harp strings are carved from the solid. She is about 4 in. (102 mm) tall, in beautiful nacre.

Fig. 33.2. A section of thick shell at the hinge, which would usually be scrapped, in Burma is turned into a graceful bird.

Fig. 33.3 (right). Quite large shells can be carved; this one from Burma is 6¼ in. (156 mm) wide, and shows a dancing girl and boy in costume, with a pagoda behind them.

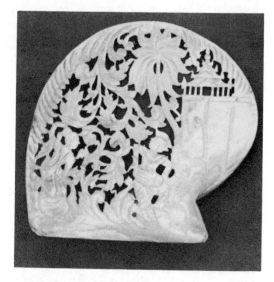

Figs. 33.4 and 33.5. Two very fine figures from Burma, both antiques which I suspect may have come from China, or at least show strong Chinese influence. One is a lady in bone, complete with fan and individually beaded multiple necklaces. (You'll have to study the sketches to get the complete idea.) She is probably a fragment and there might have been more carving at upper right. She is just as detailed on the back. With her is a monk in deer antler, again with very delicate carving around the staff and a definitely Chinese face and gown, as well as pose. The long beard conveys wisdom and holiness as well as age in China. But I found them both in Burma, near the Rangoon airport—a relatively long way from China. Each is roughly 3 in. (76 mm) tall.

Fig. 33.6. Two interesting pieces in cow legbone from Burma. One is a piper riding on a brahma cow; the other a pair of dancing ladies on a common base. The rider is 4 in. (102 mm) tall; the dancers 2⅝ in. (68 mm).

Fig. 33.7. A lady's snuff box in bone, with brass cap and base inserts and steel spatula and carrying chain, this piece is traditional Meo hill-tribe work from Thailand. The taking of snuff by women is a carryover from China.

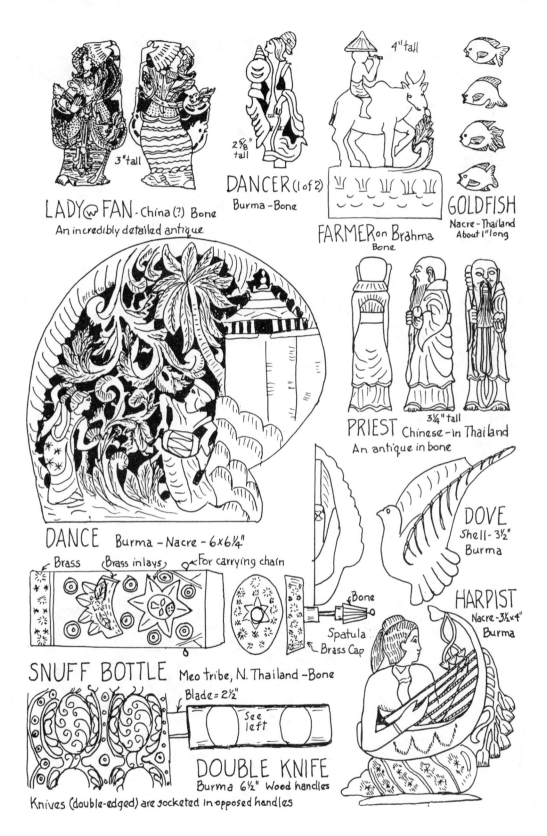

LADY w FAN - China (?) Bone
An incredibly detailed antique

DANCER (1 of 2)
Burma - Bone
2⅝" tall

4" tall

FARMER on Brahma
Bone

GOLDFISH
Nacre - Thailand
About 1" long

3" tall

PRIEST Chinese - in Thailand
An antique in bone
3¼" tall

DANCE Burma - Nacre - 6x6¼"

Brass   Brass inlays   For carrying chain

SNUFF BOTTLE Meo tribe, N. Thailand - Bone

Bone
Spatula
Brass Cap

DOVE
Shell - 3½"
Burma

HARPIST
Nacre - 3½x4"
Burma

Blade = 2½"
See left

DOUBLE KNIFE
Burma 6½" Wood handles
Knives (double-edged) are socketed in opposed handles

Fig. 33.8. Patterns.

Fig. 33.9. Various birds are carved in cow and water-buffalo horn in Thailand, some real in design, some imaginative. I was particularly taken by this eagle in water-buffalo horn, with almost the entire surface textured and utilizing the differences in color of the laminated horn. The veining of feathers was done by hand, but the base decoration was done with a hand grinder. The figure is 2¼ × 4 × 8¾ in. (57 × 102 × 220 mm), with inserted glass eyes and a separate jointed wooden base, so was probably produced in a "factory," although design is fitted to the variations of the horn.

Figs. 33.10 and 33.11. On my first visit to Ecuador, I was fascinated by the tagua nut and its carving potential. The Indians there do bust portraits, colored, in these nuts as well as making up assemblies of carved nut sections, like a 10-in. (250-mm) skeleton. But, even on a second visit there, I couldn't find the raw nut, which is called "vegetable ivory" and is about 2 in. (50 mm) in diameter with a thin brown outer skin. Otherwise it reacts just like any other ivory, although it is a bit softer than elephant or walrus dentine. So now there are nuts available here. These four faces are my experiments this far. They don't compare with the Ecuadorian pieces, but those carvers have had more experience!

Fig. 33.12. John J. Wilnoty, a Cherokee with stone carvings in the Smithsonian, did the top raven pipe in red pipestone, his son the eagle head beneath it, and Stan Toomi did the Indian head. The pendant is also by Wilnoty, Sr.

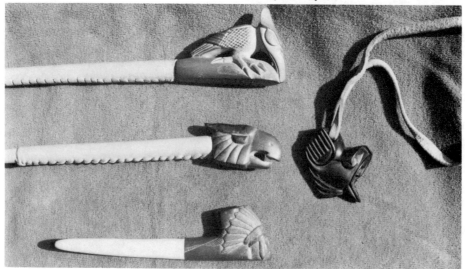

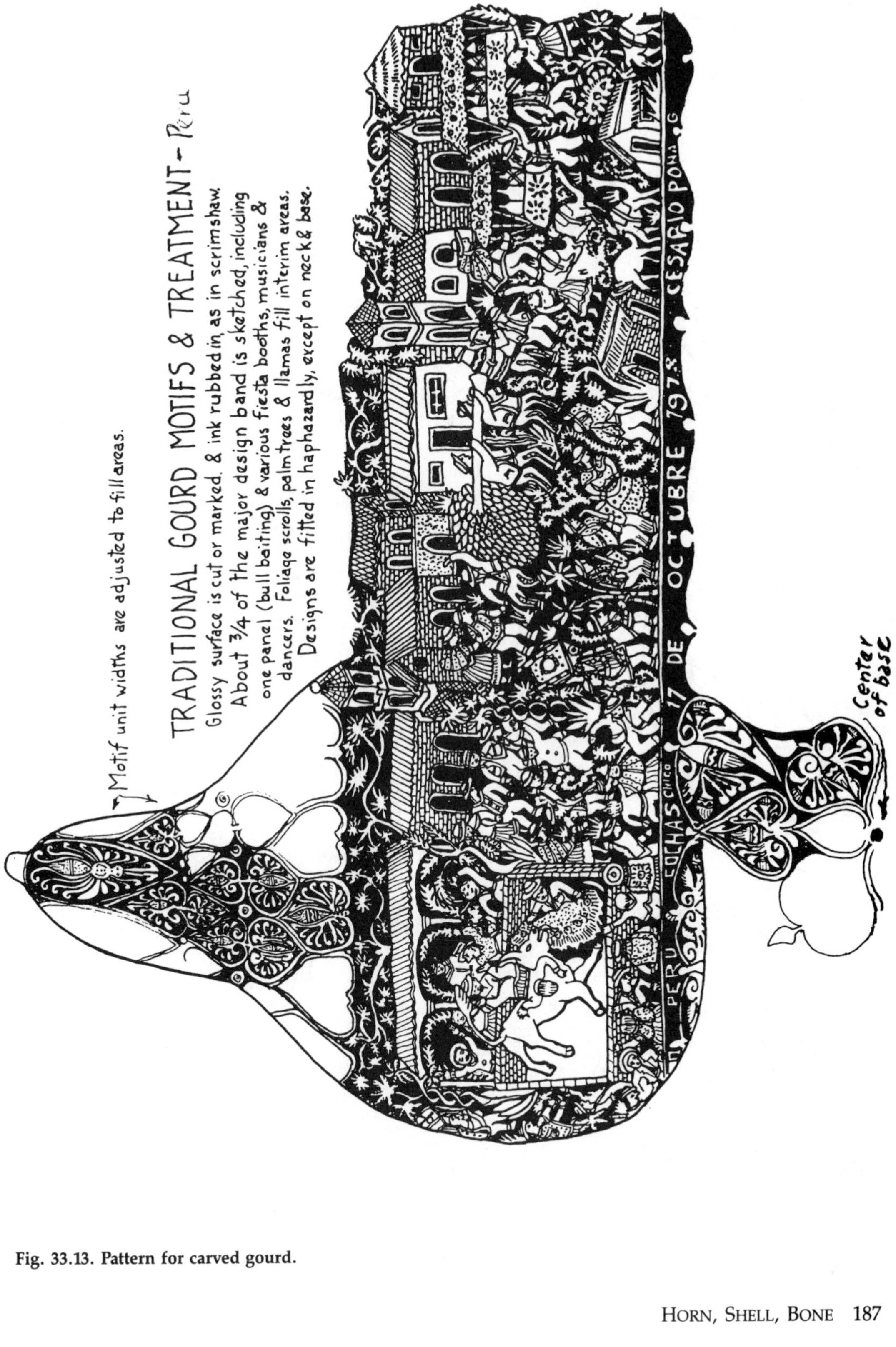
TRADITIONAL GOURD MOTIFS & TREATMENT - Peru
Glossy surface is cut or marked & ink rubbed in, as in scrimshaw.
About 3/4 of the major design band is sketched, including one panel (bull baiting) & various fiesta booths, musicians & dancers. Foliage scrolls, palm trees & llamas fill interim areas.
Designs are fitted in haphazardly, except on neck & base.
Motif unit widths are adjusted to fill areas.
Center of base
PERU
COCHAS CHICO
17 DE OCTUBRE 1978
CESARIO POMA G

Fig. 33.13. Pattern for carved gourd.

PENDANTS Soft stone or wood

TAGUA NUT LOW RELIEFS 1⅝ x 1¾"

1⅝ x 1⅞" E.J.T.

IMAGE Peru (Original in stone)

TRUMPETER Thailand - Teak (w) white-wood inserts - 2 to 6" long. A common design

White wood inserts

CHARM Thai - ⅝" long
LION - ⅜"

"TOOTH" (w) **GUARD LION** Ivory - Thai - 1½"

BUDDHA Thai - Ivory - ¾"

Feathering is very close veiner lines

SHELL BUST Italy Conch(?) core

SHELL PENDANT Italy

Orant Thai - Various woods - 1½" tall

MINIATURES Typical of many

EAGLE - Thailand - Water-buffalo horn - 2½ x 4 x 8¾"

Fig. 33.14. Patterns.

Appendix

METRIC EQUIVALENCY CHART

MM—MILLIMETRES   CM—CENTIMETRES

INCHES TO MILLIMETRES AND CENTIMETRES

INCHES	MM	CM	INCHES	CM	INCHES	CM
1/8	3	0.3	9	22.9	30	76.2
1/4	6	0.6	10	25.4	31	78.7
3/8	10	1.0	11	27.9	32	81.3
1/2	13	1.3	12	30.5	33	83.8
5/8	16	1.6	13	33.0	34	86.4
3/4	19	1.9	14	35.6	35	88.9
7/8	22	2.2	15	38.1	36	91.4
1	25	2.5	16	40.6	37	94.0
1 1/4	32	3.2	17	43.2	38	96.5
1 1/2	38	3.8	18	45.7	39	99.1
1 3/4	44	4.4	19	48.3	40	101.6
2	51	5.1	20	50.8	41	104.1
2 1/2	64	6.4	21	53.3	42	106.7
3	76	7.6	22	55.9	43	109.2
3 1/2	89	8.9	23	58.4	44	111.8
4	102	10.2	24	61.0	45	114.3
4 1/2	114	11.4	25	63.5	46	116.8
5	127	12.7	26	66.0	47	119.4
6	152	15.2	27	68.6	48	121.9
7	178	17.8	28	71.1	49	124.5
8	203	20.3	29	73.7	50	127.0

YARDS TO METRES

YARDS	METRES	YARDS	METRES	YARDS	METRES	YARDS	METRES	YARDS	METRES
1/8	0.11	2 1/8	1.94	4 1/8	3.77	6 1/8	5.60	8 1/8	7.43
1/4	0.23	2 1/4	2.06	4 1/4	3.89	6 1/4	5.72	8 1/4	7.54
3/8	0.34	2 3/8	2.17	4 3/8	4.00	6 3/8	5.83	8 3/8	7.66
1/2	0.46	2 1/2	2.29	4 1/2	4.11	6 1/2	5.94	8 1/2	7.77
5/8	0.57	2 5/8	2.40	4 5/8	4.23	6 5/8	6.06	8 5/8	7.89
3/4	0.69	2 3/4	2.51	4 3/4	4.34	6 3/4	6.17	8 3/4	8.00
7/8	0.80	2 7/8	2.63	4 7/8	4.46	6 7/8	6.29	8 7/8	8.12
1	0.91	3	2.74	5	4.57	7	6.40	9	8.23
1 1/8	1.03	3 1/8	2.86	5 1/8	4.69	7 1/8	6.52	9 1/8	8.34
1 1/4	1.14	3 1/4	2.97	5 1/4	4.80	7 1/4	6.63	9 1/4	8.46
1 3/8	1.26	3 3/8	3.09	5 3/8	4.91	7 3/8	6.74	9 3/8	8.57
1 1/2	1.37	3 1/2	3.20	5 1/2	5.03	7 1/2	6.86	9 1/2	8.69
1 5/8	1.49	3 5/8	3.31	5 5/8	5.14	7 5/8	6.97	9 5/8	8.80
1 3/4	1.60	3 3/4	3.43	5 3/4	5.26	7 3/4	7.09	9 3/4	8.92
1 7/8	1.71	3 7/8	3.54	5 7/8	5.37	7 7/8	7.20	9 7/8	9.03
2	1.83	4	3.66	6	5.49	8	7.32	10	9.14

Index